BOOTSTRAP
SELLING

The Sandler Way

BOOTSTRAP SELLING

The Sandler Way

*Or: How to own your career
and make it flourish*

BILL MORRISON

Sandler Training

Paperback: 978-0-692-46767-1
E-book: 978-0-692-46768-8

This book is dedicated to the memory of David Sandler who set the path for us all to follow and to Robert Howard, a world class sales professional, an inspiration and a friend.

CONTENTS

FOREWORD

D avid Sandler once said, "It's the person who makes a decision that makes it successful, not the decision itself." Bill Morrison's new book offers a master class for salespeople in making good business decisions ... and in being the kind of individual whose decisions consistently result in successful business outcomes.

What Bill calls "bootstrap selling" is nothing more and nothing less than selling with a sense of deep personal accountability: for one's process, one's word, and one's customer. Once those three accountabilities are in place, all kinds of amazing things become possible. This book shows how to create that kind of accountability, which the great salesperson and the great entrepreneur share.

We find that the most successful salespeople, regardless of industry, are those who create a relationship with a coach who can serve as an accountability partner and help the salesperson track his progress toward important personal goals. No book can take the place of such a coach, of course, but the lessons in bootstrap selling that Bill offers here can definitely make that relationship richer, more productive, and more rewarding for both sides.

If you familiarize yourself with each of the critical lessons in bootstrapping that appear between these covers ... and if you work with a coach to master the behaviors, attitudes, and techniques that connect to each of those lessons ... I can promise you that your sales career will move forward to a new level of productivity. Not only that, you'll become a better person in the bargain.

David H. Mattson
President and CEO, Sandler Training

INTRODUCTION

Good salespeople learn, at some point in their careers, the difference between simply doing the job and accepting the personal responsibility to produce certain results. This book is called "Bootstrap Selling" because it is all about accepting the personal responsibility for one's sales behaviors. You might have a large team around you, and you could have a great and supportive boss, but the difference between a self-starting, high-performance "bootstrap" sales professional and an order-taker is that the bootstrapper knows it is the critical two percent extra personal commitment and acceptance of responsibility that makes things happen.

Bootstrap selling is based on the idea that all sales is entrepreneurial in nature. It is the salesperson who grows the areas of a business with which he is entrusted.

The desire to succeed is only part of the bootstrapping ethos. Without personal acceptance of responsibility and commitment to take control, the best goals in the world are just words on a piece of paper.

This book is a collection of case studies in which salespeople need to either step up or step aside in sales situations. Just like in the real world, not every bootstrap selling story has a happy ending. While success is a great teacher, failure is, too.

RED LIGHTS AND GREEN LIGHTS

The reality of selling and the responsibility it brings was something I learned early. Like many people, I came to sales from another role. When I got my first sales job, I brought my old behaviors with me.

I had always been quite organized, and I had no problem with hard work. From day one in sales, I was out and about, visiting customers, checking items off my to-do lists, mastering my product knowledge and generally being a busy beaver.

My first quarterly appraisal, therefore, came as something of a shock. My boss had seen my level of activity and hadn't been hearing any cries for help, so, with other things on his plate, he had pretty much left my territory to me. When our review started, he pulled out my annual objectives and two colored pens—one green, one red.

"Traffic light pens," he called them.

"Aren't there three colors of traffic lights?" I asked.

"Not these traffic lights. In sales, things are either moving forward or they aren't. It doesn't matter why something has stopped—if it's not moving, it's not getting anywhere."

With that, my boss began working through the list of sales opportunities I was expected to deliver. I noticed my boss was not making much use of his green pen.

Almost every opportunity on the list was showing no progress. As he asked me what was happening with each item, I heard myself say the same phrase over and over again: "I'm waiting for..." I was waiting for:

- "...the technical department to answer some questions."
- "...our finance department to approve a new credit limit."
- "...a new PowerPoint from the marketing team."
- "...the customer to run a trial."

Every excuse was genuine. I had done nothing wrong, but item after item was getting a red light against it. It was the day I learned the difference between the words "effective" and "efficient."

My problem was that I had been accepting too many "maybes," too many "think it overs," and far too many "we'll let you knows."

In my defense, I thought I was doing my job. I thought my mission was to run around presenting my features, advantages, and benefits; to be polite; and to keep my prospective customers smiling. The reality that selling is all about driving progression, that it is almost entirely dependent on generating decisions, came as a bolt from the blue. Clearly, I was not living the behaviors that made decisions happen. But I was committed to changing that. From that point on, I was on the path to becoming a bootstrap salesperson.

It was not an overnight transition.

That's an important point, one I want to be sure I explain solidly before I begin this discussion with you in earnest. It would be wrong to suggest that you can make this kind of personal transformation by pinning a poster to a wall or spending a weekend reading a book. In my case, it started with the acceptance that to achieve the success and self-respect I required, I needed to get help from those who were willing and able to coach me to the level I wanted to reach. Understanding neat sales techniques intellectually was one thing; what I needed to get to the next level was a combination of practical techniques and the human element that could turn those techniques into practice. I needed someone who would support me through the learning process. I suspect you need the same thing.

With the support of some solid mentors, I found that by understanding the **techniques** that worked for me, by putting them into practice consistently as new **behaviors** and by redefining my **attitude** toward my responsibilities, I could create a steady trajectory toward higher performance and significantly higher personal income. My performance turned around.

I was happy. Just as important, my boss was happy. In fact, since I began delivering on my objectives, I was being increasingly trusted by my company with greater and greater sales objectives. In particular, my boss let me know (in his own inimitable way) that he thought I was ready to step up to a significant sales challenge.

THE NEXT CHALLENGE

The company I was working for was multinational, with the sales teams selling multiple product lines. One product—I'll call it Product X—had never gotten off the ground in my region. The salespeople before me had always provided lots of great reasons why Product X hadn't taken off yet.

My boss at that time was a man of few words. Toward the end of the annual planning cycle, he called me to his office and showed me a graph. The graph showed the tiny sales figures for Product X in my region compared to the company's other regions.

"Bill," he said, "we have just had our global business review, and I have made the commitment, on your behalf, that your region will have a sizeable and sustainable level of business with this product within twelve months."

MAKING STUFF HAPPEN

My boss did not specify what "sizeable" meant and he certainly didn't tell me how to do it, but he made it crystal clear that he expected results. As I was digesting this news, he added a phrase that turned a nightmare mission into a dream challenge. "If you need anything at all to get this done," he said, "let me know."

I felt as though I had been given a gold card to any resources I could imagine. I dived into the job with a vengeance, constantly repeating the mission I was on whenever I met an obstacle or a potential ally. Since my boss had given me a crazy mission, I had a great story to tell. The story and the goal that went with it resonated with almost everyone.

When people saw that I was serious, a strange thing happened. Because it looked to everyone that I had a plan, people started signing up to help me achieve it. While it is a universal truth that if you are not working to your own plan, you are following somebody else's, it also rings true that if you have a story that sounds like a plan, you have a pretty good chance that people might follow you.

My sales strategy evolved as people began to offer their advice and support. The main input from me was my constant focus on and repetition of the goal my boss had set for me. At the end of the year, we delivered business to my boss that was both sizeable and sustainable. In fact, almost a decade later, that business is still thriving.

With the benefit of hindsight, it is crystal clear to me the difference between my early failure in sales and later successes: the decision to accept the responsibility for business results and to create success as a bootstrapping salesperson.

THE INVESTMENT IN CHANGE

This is not to trivialize how much effort I had expended during those ten years. Change does not happen overnight, and it takes more than a wish to make big things come true. In the ten years between these two sales episodes, I had gathered a decade of experience. I had the benefit of a number of sales training programs, several good bosses had spent time investing in giving me sound advice and good guidance and, possibly most importantly, I had had the great fortune to see excellent business people in operation and had learned to replicate some of what I had seen them do.

But, even that was not the whole story. These things were all, basically, sales techniques. All across the world right now, thousands of people are sitting in sales training seminars learning some of those same techniques. For the most part, though, they will never generate value since they are unlikely to ever be applied. A huge amount of what you learn in a classroom stays in the classroom because it is not put into practice—it never leads to behavioral change.

To turn great ideas into business and personal value, let's look at a simple model we at Sandler call the "Success Triangle."

Confidence
Outlook
Responsibility

ATTITUDE

PROSPECTING
SUCCESS

TECHNIQUE

BEHAVIOR

Goals
Plans
Actions

Strategy
Preparation
Focus

The idea behind the Success Triangle is simple.

Techniques are great business tools that help move you toward your objectives more efficiently.

When you consistently apply these techniques, you have developed a new **Behavior**.

Once you make a real behavioral change, it leads to the experience and perspective to develop a new **Attitude**.

My own experience of learning how to sell was no different than that of anyone else. It revolved around a single choice—the choice to accept that I would have to change. Change meant doing things differently. Change for me is the same as change for anyone else. It revolves around understanding your comfort zone and then moving outside it. That means accepting that you need to get used to the idea of being uncomfortable.

WHAT IT TAKES

A few years ago, professional tennis player Andy Murray had become the sport's most famous runner up. He made a lot of finals, but did not pick up a lot of silverware. Then, within a few months, he had won the Wimbledon Men's Singles trophy and an Olympic Gold Medal. Of all the plaudits that flooded in, one really resonated with me: "Andy Murray made himself learn how to do things that he did not enjoy doing." That may be one of the smartest summaries ever given of what personal development requires.

The good news is that the payback is massive. Applying the new techniques you learn drives new behaviors. For me, the two critical behaviors I needed but didn't enjoy were: a commitment to displaying shocking and disarming honesty, and acting on the concept that the human being I was talking to was the center of the sales relationship.

I always had a lot to say, so slamming on the brakes and behaving as though what the other person had to say was actually more important than my sales pitch was a tough learning experience. Being open and honest enough to put my agenda on the table as being of equal value to that of the customer was something that also came as a real shock and was a tough behavior to adopt. But I did it.

ATTITUDE VS. TECHNIQUE

Some years ago the founder of the startup IT firm where I worked went on my first joint sales call with me. He was a sales nightmare—he argued with the client, spoke too much, rarely asked any questions and spent a considerable amount of time explaining to the client that their strategy was plain dumb. Amazingly, the client adored him.

Despite every apparent failure in sales technique that he displayed, his passion, honesty and joy in the subject was so transparent that everything he said sounded like music to the ears of the client. Years later I learned the phrase, "Attitude beats technique every time." I knew it to be true as soon as I heard it because I remembered that man.

One of the most common problems with developing professional skills is a dependence on "tricks and techniques." Sometimes people can learn to adopt new ideas in practice, but unless they address their attitudes, their core beliefs will rise to the surface again and they will revert to their previous way of behaving. Many salespeople have had the experience of leaving a training course full of good intentions only to find that within a few weeks they can barely remember what was covered in the training. That is why you need to understand what the winning attitudes are in sales—the bootstrapping attitudes.

BOOTSTRAP SELLING ATTITUDES

Think of any group of people you know, in any field of activity, and you will probably find that the group breaks out into three sections.

Unfortunately, there is always a group at the bottom that is going nowhere. These people focus on reasons for failure: why they have been let down by their product, their company, the clients, or even the economy. They are non-performers and probably get what they expect to get, which is failure.

In the middle there is a group I call "at-leasters": these people may not be at the top, but they wake up every morning thinking things like, "At least I'm not totally failing," or "At least I'm a little bit better than last year," or "At least there are people on the team who will get kicked out before me." Their mission is to make sure they cover their back and produce enough to stay out of harm's way.

Then there is the top group, the group of individuals who see all the same issues as the at-leasters but accept that these problems are just a natural part of their business lives.

RESPONSIBILITY

The people in the top group accept that, regardless of the challenges they face, they own the responsibility to produce results. This acceptance of responsibility is far and away the number one attitude that good salespeople need to adopt.

Bootstrap salespeople are likely to think, "If it can be done, is there any reason I can't be the one to do it? What do I need, and who can help me get it?"

They know they have a long list of tasks to complete every day, but they never lose sight of the basic question, "What have I committed to, and how do I measure myself?"

There are two parts to this: the "hard" measures of results and goals, which tend to be based on numbers, and the behavioral measures. These define the actions to be taken on a consistent basis. This is virtually the same as creating one's own personal corporate culture.

EVERYDAY BRAVERY

It would be wrong to say that applying new techniques and turning them into behaviors does not require a touch of courage. In order to turn intellectual understanding into sales value, you need to apply a measure of "everyday bravery." It's not superhero bravery; it is a small, low-risk, day-to-day type of bravery that allows you to step outside your normal limits of comfort to try a new thing. It could also be called "everyday" because you do need to do it every day. If you go a full working day without straying into new behavioral territory or into a place where you are slightly less comfortable, then you have to ask yourself, "Am I on cruise control?"

The shocking thing about slipping into cruise control for a day or so is that you can wake up six months further down the road and suddenly realize that you have just dozed your way through half a year.

The conscious effort to choose to do the tougher things has a pay-off much bigger than the immediate impact on performance. It is the one and only way to improve the real driving force of higher performance: attitude.

CHOICES

You might often hear buzzwords like "empowerment" and "ownership" in a business context, but what do they mean in a practical sense?

To salespeople who define themselves as being responsible for a critical business objective—bootstrap salespeople—it comes down to the attitude of always having, and having to make, choices.

Since everything you do and say has an impact on how your clients and prospects view you, it's best to accept the idea that you have a huge element of control over what happens next. Bootstrap salespeople have an attitude of never being out of the decision zone. If you are not reviewing your options and making conscious decisions, you are not thinking, you are not taking risks, and you are not using your intellect to work out what your options are.

DAY ONE MENTALITY

Do you remember your first day of a new sales responsibility? The day when you had nothing left to do except go out there and meet your customers and prospects face-to-face or pick up the phone to find new people to pitch?

In most cases you were likely to have some history to work with: existing clients, perhaps some live opportunities in the pipeline, hopefully a few leads to pursue. One thing is almost certain—you looked at your area of responsibility, to some extent, as a blank canvas. What were your opportunities, your roadblocks, your options? They were wide open.

Bootstrap selling relies on never losing that fresh perspective—the thought that every day in sales is Day One. Yesterday's triumphs and disasters do not define what will happen tomorrow.

If you were meeting your biggest, most established customer for the first time, what would your objectives be? How would you assess your opportunities and risks?

If someone else took over your sales responsibilities tomorrow, how would they move forward?

Bootstrap selling does not mean you change direction every day, but it does demand that you focus on your goals and regard almost everything that you do as another tool to achieve them.

PERSPECTIVE

A final element of the bootstrap-selling attitude is the realization that selling is not a war; the world is happy for you to succeed. You sell and get paid for solving the pains of your customers. I once heard this summarized by a very experienced sales leader in a way that I have copied countless times ever since. He said to a problem client, "All we want is to discover if you have a problem that we are well-suited to resolve. If you do, and if it makes sense for us both economically, then we should probably work out how to do it. If not, then it makes sense for us all to do something else with our time."

That perspective and technique are at the heart of bootstrap selling.

CHAPTER 1

A Bootstrapping Profession

Selling is, at heart, an entrepreneurial activity, which is to say it is a bootstrapping profession.

If clients and prospects do not need your help to redefine what their problems and pains are, they do not need salespeople.

Selling calls on you to go into your market and introduce an element of disruptive positive change in the lives of your clients.

In virtually every successful relationship you have with a client, you bring value to them because you guide them from having an understanding of a general "surface pain"—a symptom

> *Selling calls on you to go into your market and introduce an element of disruptive positive change in the lives of your clients.*

1

that something needs to change—to a deeper awareness of the business impact of that pain. Finally, you assist with the realization of the personal effects that come from having this pain resolved. This is what bootstrapping entrepreneurs do for their customers: they transform perceptions, identify the impacts of the status quo, and assume responsibility for adding value by challenging the status quo. It's what bootstrapping salespeople do, too.

I wrote this book to help salespeople who don't yet think of themselves as bootstrappers to think a little differently about who they are, what they do, and why they're in the game. I wrote it to help them make a difference in the lives of others—by changing how they think about themselves.

CREATING THE DIFFERENCE

Salespeople are always striving to make sure there is plenty of clear blue water between themselves and the competition. After all, if you can't separate yourselves from the "other guys," then how can you hope to command a premium in pricing or defend yourself from the competition when they try to displace you?

How should you create and sustain this competitive distance? You can get a lot of support from marketing or branding activities, but that's not the final answer, is it? Bootstrap sellers know this. Time and again, the factor that creates the critical differentiation is how salespeople personally behave in front of their customers when no one else is watching.

> *The factor that creates the critical differentiation is how salespeople personally behave in front of customers when no one is watching.*

Do you behave like the sort of person with whom your clients want to do business? Do you display the techniques, behaviors and attitudes that a bootstrapping entrepreneur would?

Here's what bootstrap salespeople have learned: behavior and attitude are vital business resources, and, like other business resources, they have to be managed carefully.

LEADING INDICATORS

Most sales activity is managed retrospectively. Success is measured by results, but since today's results are a consequence of what happened days, weeks or months previously, often what's being examined is what happened in the past, not what will happen today and tomorrow. Such sales numbers are "trailing indicators"—they come at the end of a long sales process.

To ensure that you generate sustainable success in real time, manage your "leading indicators." Those are the things that show you what is likely to happen for the next set of sales results. These leading indicators are the sales behaviors in play. To manage those indicators, you need to be able to identify the ones that drive success and the ones that can get you into trouble.

As a Sandler® trainer, I often work with sales teams to help them visualize what these behaviors look like. No two are exactly the same, but the following list is a pretty good sampling of what we find. Notice that they break down into two distinct categories.

AT-LEASTER BEHAVIORS	BOOTSTRAPPING BEHAVIORS
At-Leasters:	Bootstrappers:
• Watch the phone hoping it will ring.	• Get on the phone.
• Constantly check emails waiting for good news.	• Work to a target.
• Wait for things to happen.	• Are resilient when things do not go to plan.
• Are easily satisfied.	• Do not take rejection personally.
• Are content to beat the minimum.	• Make efficient and effective use of time.
• Have low expectations.	• Get a buzz from success and celebrate.
• Have no goals.	• Are competitive with others and with themselves.
• Have no "need to succeed."	• Are hungry to beat their goals.
• Coast through the day.	• Have a need to succeed.
• "Go dark" during tougher times.	• Display assertiveness.
• Stay in their comfort zone.	• Possess a dash of aggression.
• Follow a process too blindly without thinking about the real problem they are trying to solve for the client.	• Consistently follow a process.
• Procrastinate.	• Have strong self-belief.
• Make excuses, say "my diary is empty," and have no leads.	• Take risks.
• Rationalize failure.	• Frequently move outside their comfort zone.
• Visualize failure.	• Are "lateral thinkers" when they face a new problem.
• Stress out.	• Put in the hard hours up front.
	• Get referrals.
	• Relate to prospects as people.
	• Create strong personal relationships.
	• Delegate effectively.
	• Relax.

THE BOOTSTRAPPING DIFFERENCE

The real difference between bootstrappers and the rest of the world is not that they transform themselves into sales superheroes, but that they accept the responsibility for constant self-leadership.

Bootstrappers accept the personal responsibility to critically examine their own sales behaviors and make the constant corrections that keep them on course.

They recognize when they are doing it right and when they allow themselves to slip. (It happens!) They don't just focus on the results of their sales meetings. Like professional athletes, they critically evaluate every aspect of their own performance, regardless of the outcome.

Everyone who has sold for any length of time knows about those times when the results just aren't showing up. Sometimes this is called a "slump." Most also have the experience of pulling themselves out of that difficult period and getting back on track. But what if you could stop a slump before it happened?

That's what bootstrappers learn to do. They do it by identifying at-leaster behavior and replacing it with behavior that supports their goals. The reason I focus on negative as well as positive behaviors in this book is to give you a better chance of catching any at-leaster behavior and taking action with the techniques and behaviors that will work for you.

To do this, you need both measures of great behavior and a clear understanding of what at-leaster behavior looks like. If you fail to recognize what a mistake looks like, you are almost certainly doomed to repeat it.

> *If you fail to recognize what a mistake looks like, you are almost certainly doomed to repeat it.*

At-leaster behaviors serve as a set of warning signs. If you allow yourself to fall into these patterns, your results further down the line are bound to be negative.

YARDSTICKS

In this book, I aim to illustrate clear examples of both bootstrapping behavior and at-leaster behavior through a series of short case studies. Each story has been written to show the impact of behavior on outcomes.

I decided to use this approach because people learn from experience, and experience is best shared using stories. If experience is the best way to learn, the smartest way to get that experience is probably to learn from someone else's.

In each of these stories you will see sales professionals make decisions, or sometimes fail to make decisions, that have a major impact on results.

TAKE ACTION

Think back to your own most memorable experiences in sales, both the successes and the failures. Take a moment to write down what happened. What decisions did you take or not take? What options did you have, and did you pursue them? Were you in a position in which five seconds of everyday bravery would have paid off? What did you do at the moment of truth?

We at Sandler call this process "journaling." Many top performers adopt this as a technique.

Journaling should become a habit for anyone who wants to put himself onto a pathway of dramatically improving his performance. It is a simple task that revolves around recording some key points on a daily basis, such as:

- What did I do today that drove my business forward?
- What should I have done differently?
- What was the least comfortable thing I did today?
- Why did someone buy from me?
- Why did someone choose not to work for me, and what could I have done about that?

The more you make this a daily habit, the more effective it will be for you.

My challenge to you, as you work through the chapters that follow, is to take note of the key learning points from each one and think of times when you either fell into some of the traps described or when you used some of these bootstrapping techniques, maybe without even knowing it.

Write it all down!

Learn from this book—and use this book to learn from your own past experiences.

CHAPTER 2

Lessons from the Worst Salesman in the World

Or: An at-leaster learns some basics

There are two motivations for any sales dialogue with a prospect: the salesperson's reason to sell and the prospect's reason to buy. The two are not to be confused. I was lucky enough to learn this tough lesson early in my career, but not without a little pain on my side.

According to those who don't know any better, the responsibility of a salesperson is to persuade people to buy whatever he happens to be selling. "He could sell ice to an Eskimo" is supposedly the highest compliment to a salesperson—the idea being that a great sale meets the needs of the salesperson regardless of whether the customer actually needs it.

The reality is that the only sale that really sticks is the one that is driven by the needs of the customer.

Here's another reality: the best way to find out what that customer needs is to go straight to the horse's mouth and ask.

Effective salespeople learn this lesson. Others don't, and continue to underachieve. If you are lucky, you learn the lesson early in your career. If you are unlucky, you never learn it at all. Apparently, there is a fair number of unlucky salespeople out there.

For all too many salespeople, the motto seems to be, "Keep pitching until they surrender." You meet a lot of salespeople who live by this motto, even though they have ample personal experience demonstrating the mediocrity of the results this approach generates. Many "senior" salespeople seem to have 20 or so years of experience, when in fact they have had one year's experience 20 or so times.

> *The only sale that really sticks is the one that is driven by the needs of the customer.*

Since the focus of this book is to learn from the mistakes of others, it seems only fair that I jump in first with a disaster story of my own.

ON THE ROAD

My own first sales job was working for a book wholesaler. We didn't publish anything; we bought books in bulk at the end of their normal print runs and discounted them to retailers at bargain prices. Our titles tended to be at the popular end of the market, mostly large format books on popular subjects with a lot of illustrations.

After I spent a week or two learning the ropes in the warehouse and the invoicing department, my boss Trevor took me out on the road to meet a real live customer for the first time. Trevor had seen and done pretty much everything in the book industry and was a hard guy to impress. I was determined to blow his socks off with my natural sales ability.

In order to get one step ahead of Trevor, I went to the warehouse manager and asked him for a list of the top-selling books we stocked. I made sure those sure-fire winners were right on top of the enormous sample bag I had to carry.

Our first call was in a small town near our office, with a buyer who had been a customer for years. The store sold toys, some kids' clothes, and some books, most of which came from us.

Trevor checked me out before we left. "Do you have a catalogue, a pen, and an order pad?" he asked. I did. That was it. I was good to go.

The shop owner was a very nice lady who offered salespeople a cup of coffee and liked to chat for a while before getting down to business. Being the total hot shot I was, I decided to leave the time-wasting chit-chat to Trevor. The idea of investing time and effort into creating a bond with the client and creating good rapport was totally alien to me. As the gossip portion of the meeting seemed to be winding down, I decided that it was time to launch my killer moves.

> My first shot at a benefit sale was going nowhere.

THE KILLER PITCH

"Let me show you what is really selling right now," I said enthusiastically, pulling out the best-selling book we had in the whole warehouse, *Hitler's Panzer Armies of World War II*. "This is a great seller, everyone else is buying tons of this title. You could move a lot of copies of this. You should order now before we sell out."

The lady smiled, "Well, Bill, this is a children's store. We sell to kids and their parents. So we only stock children's books."

I was stumped.

Before starting the job, I had bought a book on sales. I had learned all about selling through pitching features, advantages, and benefits, but my first shot at a benefit sale was going nowhere. "OK, how about this?" I said. "Our warehouse manager tells me that this is almost flying out the door. It's a real money maker." I showed her my sample of yet another book targeted at the adult market, *Horrible Murders of Old London Town*.

She was polite enough to pretend to look at the blood-spattered cover of the book for a second before handing it back to me.

"Hmm," she said. "Mainly we just sell picture books, puzzle books, that sort of thing, and we're just interested in children's books. You see, if we sell books, then parents might come in to pick up a book and end up buying something else—toys or whatever. "

CRASHING AND BURNING

My first customer ever was simply refusing to work with me. I jammed the sample back into my bag, reaching for the next sure-fire winner. By this time, Trevor was staring at me with a mixture of amazement and curiosity. He had actually moved around to the customer's side of the counter to get a spectator's perspective on my catastrophic performance.

I reached into my bag and pulled out number three on our top-seller list. Surely she could not possibly turn me down on *The History of Torture*—a real winner if there ever was one.

Trevor saw what I was reaching for and put his hand on my arm to stop me. "Bill, why don't you wait for me in the car?"

Many people have been thrown out of a sales meeting by a client, but I think I have the unique distinction of being thrown out of my very first sales call by my own boss. I sat in the car for half an hour while Trevor calmed the client down and then took a reasonable order for kids' books.

FIRST LESSON

Eventually, Trevor joined me in the car. He patiently asked, "Bill, how do you find out what a customer wants to buy?"

I thought I had learned my lesson. "You look to see what kind of things they already stock?"

"Nope."

"You check to see what they have bought before?"

"Nope."

"You look at what other shops like theirs have bought and sell those?"

"Nope."

After a long silence I suspected that my sales career was over. It was 10:30 in the morning on my first day on the road. "I give up," I said.

"Well," Trevor said, "you ask them, you idiot."

This felt too easy. I objected, "Isn't that cheating?"

Trevor looked into the distance and wondered what he had done to deserve a salesman this dumb. "No, Bill. Selling people things they want to buy is not cheating. It's called *selling*. Have you ever heard about walking a mile in someone else's shoes?"

> *"Selling people things that they want to buy is not cheating."*

Believe it or not, I had never heard that phrase. And the idea of trying to see the world from the side of the customer had never entered my mind.

LESSON LEARNED

Trevor was nice enough not to fire me, but it was some time before I was allowed to fly solo. Eventually, I was allowed out on my own. Trevor's checklist had expanded from the original, "Do you have a catalogue, a pen, and an order pad?" to include this final item: "What is the first question you are going to ask the customer?"

I learned the right answer. "I am going to ask what kind of books he wants to buy." Trevor would nod, but it took him a while before his confidence in me returned.

One of the great truths of selling is that telling isn't selling. Like most novice salespeople, I had assumed that my mission was to convince people to do what I wanted. I would tell them what made sense and convince them to follow my stunning plan. Unfortunately, many, many salespeople spend years in their role without progressing past this novice stage.

> *The salesperson's job is not to get meetings.*

Customers all over the world are trapped every day in endless presentations about products and services they don't need with salespeople from whom they never plan to buy. Why? Because the salesperson fails to qualify what is on the customer's "must do" list. Millions are spent on travel every year by sales teams jetting across the world to pitch great ideas that will never get off the ground, simply because they remain clueless about the customer's true agenda.

The salesperson's job is not to get meetings, not to organize presentations or site visits, and not to write killer sales proposals. It is to find out what the customer needs and to identify those customers who have a need that fits the salesperson's offer.

It is easy to forget that the simplest and fastest opportunity to sell comes when you are selling something the customer already wants to buy. The one best place to start the discovery process is asking the customer what that is.

IN THE ZONE

For weeks, my sales calls were pretty much identical. "Hello. I am Bill from the book company. What sort of books do you think you might want to buy?" The customer who had a pretty good idea about what made his business tick would say something like: "We like books about cooking and so forth." I would dive into my sample bag and say: "Here you are, this one is all about cooking. Is it something you would want to stock?" Very often the customer would. In fact I became good at selling books, so I was pretty cocky when Trevor said he would come out on the road with me for a day.

Our first call that day was at a classic car museum. "Hi! I'm Bill from the book company. What kinds of books are selling well for you right now?"

"Oh, you know, books about old cars mainly," said the museum manager wondering why someone was asking such a stupid question.

"Great!" I said. "We have some of those. Do you think you might want to buy some?"

After showing him our books about classic cars and getting the order, I threw in my killer punch. "Do people ever come in here who are not very interested in old cars, children being pulled along by their parents for example? You could sell some kids' books."

The manager thought for a second and then said, "Why not? We can give it a try."

THE GREATEST SALESMAN IN THE WORLD

So we sold the car museum some children's books and I crowned myself the Greatest Salesman in the World. Back in the car with

Trevor I could not contain myself with triumph, "Did you see that, Trevor? I got him there. He had never thought of selling kids' books. I sure showed him."

Trevor looked at me with genuine sympathy. "Bill, you need to understand something very important—we are on the same side as our customers. We are not out to beat them."

This was nothing short of a revelation to me—wasn't selling all about winning, being one step ahead of the customers? They had a big bag of money and we had a warehouse full of product. The objective was to manipulate them into giving us the money in exchange for the product. It was a war, or so I had thought.

By this time, I think Trevor had begun to see me as an interesting challenge, a bit like a one-person remedial sales class.

> *"We are on the same side as our customers.*
> *We are not out to beat them."*

"Bill," he said, "what we want is for our customers to be successful. We like it if they think we might be just a little bit responsible for their success."

This made sense. "So we have to pretend to care about their business?" I said.

Trevor knew how to accept small victories. "That will be a start, Bill. Let's work with that for now."

WHO WINS?

There are two ways to look at sales: one is to see selling as a conflict where one side wins and the other loses, and the other is to recognize that the sales job is to support customers in making the right decisions *for them*. Ideally, that decision will include buying from you because you have qualified the customer correctly in the first place. If it turns out that you can't help the customer, and if you (not the customer) say so first, you will probably have made the best investment in your sales career by telling the truth under pressure.

Trevor stuck with me, which was remarkable in itself. After about six months, I hit my stride. I now had what I thought were two of the most devastating weapons in the history of sales. First, I would ask people questions about what they wanted to buy from me instead of talking about my product. Second, I would show some concern about their business. I had even grown to the point that the concern was genuine.

Armed with these two principles, I became a slightly better salesperson, and sold some books.

My guess is that the lion's share of all salespeople around the world have still not learned those two principles. They are flying around desperately, pitching products to clients without asking about what might be on their agenda and not showing the slightest interest in the success of their business.

SANDLER TAKEAWAYS FOR BOOTSTRAPPERS

1. **People buy from people they like, and they like people who are a little bit like themselves.** Failing to invest in creating a bond and establishing a rapport with clients is one of the biggest sales killers in the world. Your products and services are simply the means by which your clients resolve the pains they are experiencing. You need to put yourself in the shoes of your prospects to understand the value you can create for them.

2. **Sell what customers want to buy, not what you want to sell.** People love to buy, but they hate being "sold." In practice, this might sound confusing, but here's an example. Let's say you're

selling into retail. You may think you are selling your great product, your fantastic pricing strategy, your creative brand, and your tip-top customer service. In fact what a retailer buys is probably more along the lines of the most profitable way to use shelf space.

3. **Telling isn't selling.** Being able to point out the great advantages of whatever you are selling is great. Having a super snappy presentation created by your friends in the marketing department is terrific. Yet telling people what you want to sell them is much, much less than half the battle. As generations of teachers and grandparents have advised: "You have two ears and one mouth, so use them in that proportion and in that order."

4. **You and the prospect are on the same side.** This is controversial. A lot of salespeople see themselves as hunters, as rock-star rainmakers who "win" every time they deal with customers. Financial traders think like this. They sell breathtakingly complex derivatives and bonds that literally cannot be explained and that often have a disturbing tendency to become close to worthless shortly after they are sold. I don't care how much money there is to be made—I won't sell like that, and you shouldn't either. Sooner or later, it backfires. If you see selling as a game where one side wins at the expense of the other, you are riding for a fall—and are probably in the wrong job.

CHAPTER 3

Heavy Lifting

Or: How a bootstrapper finds out the reason to buy

There is only one reason that people buy, and this is to resolve a Pain. Even when every message they send is positive, you need to keep digging until you truly understand what the pain is that is motivating them.

This is the situation Joe, a salesperson with a heavy lifting equipment manufacturer, faced when he worked with a prospect who looked good—on paper. "The client is very engaged," Joe told his VP of marketing. "He is asking a lot of great questions, working on a detailed business case to support this purchase and giving us almost complete access to the company's senior people as well as the operational team. In other words, this deal has all the hallmarks of a disaster waiting to happen."

But then Joe smiled.

"Joe, how can you say that this looks like a disaster?" Nadia, the VP, was almost out of her chair. "This client ticks every box. We couldn't wish for a better prospect than this."

"After 15 years in this business," Joe said, "I have never seen a major deal going through that did not hit at least one sizeable bump in the road. This one looks too good to be true. If something looks too good, then I am inclined to say that it may actually be too good."

"So you think we should go looking for problems?" Nadia asked.

TOO GOOD TO BE TRUE?

"Actually," Joe said, "that's precisely what I think we need to do. Until we pressure-test this thing, I am going to keep my skeptical hat on. I'm not going to project income against quota from this lead. I know the company seems to want to do this deal, but I am still not convinced that we understand why they need it. Working with us will cost them well over a million in just the first year. Experience suggests that somebody, somewhere, inside their organization is eventually going to push back on the idea. We have no idea how the happy campers we're talking to inside the client team will react to that pressure, and we have no idea from where the pressure will come. We need to understand their personal motivation to keep going when the tough questions get asked."

> *"We need to find out their personal motivation."*

Nadia thought for a few minutes, going back over the client meetings she had attended. Joe was right. There had been nothing but good news and happy faces on every trip. That did seem a little odd. Maybe Joe was right. "So we need to find out their personal motivation, to understand what is driving this whole thing at a higher level. What is the strategy to get to that sort of information?"

"I only ever have one plan for that sort of thing," said Joe. "If I want to get information that the client has, I fall back on an old sales trick: I ask."

Two weeks later, Nadia and Joe traveled to the client site to sit down with Harry, the head of operations, and Clem, the director responsible for equipment. The firm in question was one of the best-known players in the world of heavy lifting. People knew them for huge cranes bearing the company logo, visible on major construction sites across the country, However, most of the firm's revenue came from static and semi-mobile lifting systems, the kind of machine that can lift a railway engine or massive earthmover on and off a low loader.

WHY BUY?

The rationale behind Joe's deal came from the client's marine engineering division. As far as Joe and Nadia understood it, the client needed a mobile crane with long reach that could move up to 1,000 tons, but would still only take up a small footprint and could operate in tight spaces. If they had the equipment to do this, they could do more work on ships without having to use expensive dry dock space.

Joe set the meeting up with a very limited agenda. The discussion was intended to allow everyone to step back a little, take stock, and evaluate where the relationship was going.

"Harry, Clem," Joe said, "I want to thank you for making the time for this meeting. From our side, we'd like to get an overview of how you see this project, to map out next steps and to let each of us share our issues and concerns. Speaking personally, my biggest concern is that we might be getting a little lost in the weeds. I think we are still unclear about how you see this whole project working out for your business. I'm sure you have your own questions, as well. I was thinking we could use today to explore those questions. Does that kind of discussion work for you?"

> *"Has anything changed since the last time we met?"*

"It sure does," answered Clem. "It's good to take a little time out on something as big as this."

"Is there anything special from your side you want to cover?" Joe asked. "Has anything changed since the last time we met?"

"Everything is still much the same as the last time we spoke."

"Great. You know, typically when we have this sort of chat, we do a review of the project plan, the dates and action, and we then send it over to you to make sure we are on the same page. Does that make sense?"

"We're good with that, Joe," Harry said. "What's on your mind?"

BACK TO BASICS

Joe jumped right in. "If you don't mind, I would like to go back to basics. We understand that by using our new Super Heavy, you will be able to do work at dockside rather than working in dry docks, and that can reduce costs significantly. Dockside work is cheaper than dry dock, is that right?"

"Good question," said Clem. "While it looks cheaper to work in a dry dock because everything you need is right there at hand, the time involved in getting in and out of the dock and the time wasted waiting for a berth to be free is the real cost driver."

"Oh, thanks for that," Joe said. "I missed that point in our earlier meetings. So it is the lost time that causes the cost issue. Could you expand on that a little? Tell me more about that."

> **"Could you give me an example?"**

"Dry docks tend not to be in exactly the right places compared to where the ships travel to on a daily basis. The ships have to schlep up and down the coast to get to the right yard."

"I get it," Joe said. "Could you give me an example?"

DIGGING DOWN

Harry and Clem laughed.

"We could probably fill a book with examples," said Harry. "Let me tell you about a project we just finished. We needed to replace the main shaft in a mid-size container ship. Of the total cost to the shipping line, almost two-thirds came from lost time, both from travel and from waiting for the dry dock to be available. Ships need to be working flat out to cover their costs."

"We know a lot about lifting, but not as much about marine engineering," said Joe. "If I happened to own a container ship and need a new shaft, how much would that set me back?"

"Let me just say you're not going to get any change from $200,000."

"Wow," Joe said. "And the lost time was double that? I can see the issue. Doing things without dry docking makes a lot of sense, but you must have looked at other options before now, correct?"

"Sure, we did. There are at least two other ways to do this. One is a floating dry dock and the other is a floating crane. Both work, technically, but both are tougher to move and neither of them can be used on land, which is what we would want your machine to do."

"I suppose you must have run some sort of cost analysis on those options?" asked Joe.

"Joe, we don't want to tell you all our little secrets," said Clem, smiling, "but I can say that this idea of yours should be able to shave at least 20 percent off our heavy lifting costs."

"So the whole thing revolves around cost?"

ALL ABOUT THE COST?

"Cost is critical, of course," said Harry, "but let me tell you the real driver here. This is a tough market. Marine engineering is incredibly competitive right now, and this idea could give us a competitive edge."

"I know exactly what you mean," said Nadia. "Getting an edge in a heavy engineering market can be a real challenge."

"What is your biggest concern over this project?"

"You don't have to tell us how tough this business is on cost," said Harry.

"How long have you been looking for a way to differentiate yourselves from the rest of the market like this? Is this a new initiative?" Joe asked. "It must be pretty frustrating trying to fight on price."

Clem and Harry laughed. "Yes, 'frustrating' is a reasonable word for it," Clem said. "We have looked at a few ideas over the past year, but this concept seems to be the only one that stands up to scrutiny."

"If you don't mind me asking, what is your biggest concern over this project?"

DIGGING DEEPER

Joe noticed a change in Harry's body language. He leaned forward over the desk and looked closely at Joe.

"Joe, since you ask," Harry said, "there is one thing that still worries us. Right now our biggest concern is the possibility that your side does not deliver. We have had suppliers in here who made some pretty strong promises, then decided after they got the deal that they couldn't actually walk the talk. Clem and I have both pushed this pretty hard internally. If you suddenly feel that you don't like some part of the idea after all, we are going to be left high and dry."

There was an uncomfortable silence in the room. Nadia was the first to speak.

"I really appreciate you sharing that with us," she said, "so here is what we will do. When we get back to the office, and we will go over the whole proposal again in detail with the team, and then we will sit down with our CEO and CFO to make sure they are fully comfortable with every aspect of it. Once we have their blessing on what we've done, we will get it right over to you. Ideally, you can get back to us with your timeline from here to contract signature. Does that make sense?"

"I'll tell you what makes even more sense," said Harry, "Once you have that all checked on your side, you should get your CEO to call our CEO and have the two of them talk it through. Might be good to start building that bridge now rather than later."

"Sounds like an excellent plan," Joe said. "Give us until the middle of next week, and we will look at setting up that call."

A few hours later Nadia and Joe were on the flight home.

"Now are you happy?" asked Nadia.

Joe smiled. "Well, I'm still a skeptic. Let's say I am less unhappy. Quite a lot less."

SANDLER TAKEAWAYS FOR BOOTSTRAPPERS

1. **No pain, no sale.** It's easy for a salesperson to be blinded by how much he believes in what he is selling. The prospect does not always have the same vision of what can be done as the salesperson does. If the prospect seems to be moving quickly toward a sale, the salesperson will think, "Of course, it's fast; our stuff is great." But no matter how great the sales strategy is, if the real pain has not been uncovered, the strategy is built on hope and luck, not a solid sales process.

2. **Pain has three levels.** Settling for a brief description of the pain the solution can address is one of the cardinal sins of sales. Too often salespeople try to close on a "surface pain." To get into the shoes of prospects, you need to dig down deeper. The next level is to find out the *business impact* of the pain. Why do anything at all? Why are they not sticking with the status quo? Once you know that, you can refocus on the principle, "People buy from people." What is the *personal stake* here?

3. **Your first idea about where pain resides is nearly always wrong.** If the customer was always right, the world would not need salespeople. Prospects could buy everything they needed over the Internet or through a bidding process. Salespeople thrive because the true job is to help the prospect uncover the pain underneath the surface.

4. **Your job is to be brave enough to voice your "biggest concern."** If you are honest with yourself, you will admit that, at least once in nearly every sale, you get that nagging feeling that something is a little wrong. Every salesperson has that feeling, but often there's not enough everyday bravery prompting the tough question that gets to the truth. Prospects are looking for a partner who can solve their pains for them. Good partners are not afraid to raise the tough issues.

CHAPTER 4

Pete's Question

Or: An at-leaster learns to see the world from the prospect's perspective

Salespeople love to talk—especially about the product knowledge they possess.

Why is this so? Simple. Selling often feels difficult, or even inappropriate. If you can fill the time during a meeting talking about neutral, painless things such as the technical issues related to products and services, that can feel comforting.

Take Marcus. He knew a lot about his product, but not nearly as much as he should have about why a prospect should buy from him. Like a lot of other salespeople, Marcus came into the world with two ears and one mouth. As I mentioned before, that ratio is worth considering closely. If you are trying to use your ears and mouth in their correct proportion, then everything you say should have a purpose—uncovering the facts behind the customer's problem.

There are entire selling systems built on the art and science of questioning techniques, but often they miss the one big question that counts: Pete's Question.

> *Use your ears and mouth in their correct proportion.*

Marcus met Pete quite early in his sales career. Like a lot of people, Marcus went into sales as a graduate trainee. From being a normal, scruffily dressed student, Marcus was transformed into a proper white-collar salesperson and equipped with a regulation blue suit, a dark tie, and a shiny new briefcase (which his mother bought him). Because he was a junior salesperson, he was given an important job title: "Territory Business Development Executive." He loved it.

Marcus worked for a major chemicals company. In fact, he and the other new salespeople were taught to say that they were in the world's "top 11" chemical companies (making them probably number 11 on that list).

On joining the firm, Marcus spent three solid months learning everything you could ever need to know about the firm's products. He knew how long they lasted; how they worked; what was in them; and where, when, and why they could be used. At the end of that three months, Marcus knew everything—or thought he did. He had successfully completed a product training marathon of epic proportions.

Shortly after that long-term induction period, Marcus was unleashed on the world. The company sent him to ride along with one of the more experienced salespeople in the company—Pete.

PRODUCT KNOWLEDGE

On their first day out in the field, Pete and Marcus drove through an industrial section of Marcus's brand new territory. Pete pointed to a building under construction and asked Marcus which of their chemical systems should be used on the framework.

"Why, that's easy," said Marcus, who was proud of his product knowledge. "We would use our environmentally friendly Blah de Blah product first of all, then our Super-Dooper Umpty-Ump System, and then coat everything with Whatcha-Callit Extra."

Pete, who had somehow managed to hide how impressed he was with Marcus's technical knowledge, looked puzzled. "Hmmm," Pete replied. "Why would you use all that stuff?"

"What do you mean?" Marcus asked, shocked at the question. "It's the best on the market! It's cutting edge! It's low-impact!"

Then he got Pete's Question: "So what?"

This was a question that Marcus's product training hadn't covered. Marcus was speechless—but only for a moment.

SO WHAT?

"'So what?'" squeaked Marcus. "What do you mean, 'So what?' It's the best on the market."

"So what?"

Surely being the very best product on the market was reason enough? "So it's tougher," Marcus said.

"So what?"

"So it lasts longer."

"So what?"

"So you don't have to worry about it failing."

"So what?"

Marcus thought. Then he smiled. "So you can leave it for a long time without having to maintain it."

Pete persisted: "So what?"

A dim light was dawning in Marcus's eyes. "Ah! If you use all our super products you reduce your maintenance costs. Right?"

"You tell me," Pete said.

"People should use our stuff because it cuts maintenance costs," Marcus said.

Now it was Pete's turn to smile. "So if people buy our high specification expensive products today," Pete said, patiently, "they will be able to save money on maintenance in about five years' time? Is that what you're saying?"

"I suppose so," Marcus answered.

Pete was guiding Marcus past the features trap, the place where at-leasters go to die. He had done that with a single, startlingly simple question: "So what?"

> *Getting past the features trap is one of the biggest steps you can take toward becoming a bootstrap salesperson.*

"Let me ask you something," Pete said. "Do you think the person who's putting the building up is the same person who's going to be using it in five years' time?"

Marcus had covered this point in his induction training. "Nope," he said, his face beaming with confidence. "Once the building's finished, it will be passed on to some building managers."

"So if I tell the construction company that our expensive products will cut somebody else's maintenance costs in five years, what do you think they're going to say to me?"

There was a little silence. "They will probably say 'So what?'" said Marcus. His face was no longer so confident.

Pete nodded. "So let's work out what we are going to say when the customer asks us that question: 'So what?'"

Marcus thought for a moment. Pete navigated the curves in the road like the expert he was, and the car moved steadily forward.

After about a quarter of a mile, Marcus said: "Using our stuff keeps you out of trouble with all those environmental regulators who love to make life a nightmare for construction companies."

"Interesting," Pete said, his eyes on the road. "Tell me more."

Now both of them were smiling.

Here's the point. A product, service, policy, or idea being great is only a starting point. Everything you sell, without exception, is subject to the "So what?" test, no matter how great the product is. Asking Pete's Question ahead of time is the salesperson's job. It is everyone else's job to think about great new ideas—but the only people who need to care about what the products do from the customers' point of view are the sales team and the CEO.

Pete's Question takes you past the features trap—one of the biggest steps you can take toward becoming a bootstrap salesperson. The simple act of asking, "So what?" to every clever thing your company does will bring the real benefits you are selling into focus—and help you change your selling message so that it matches up with the world of the prospect.

SANDLER TAKEAWAYS FOR BOOTSTRAPPERS

1. **Stop guessing.** If you really don't know for sure exactly what goal you will help customers achieve or what bad thing you will help them avoid, you are guessing. Note: Very often, the thing you are selling can be used as a tool to solve several different problems for your customer.

2. **Product knowledge is both a blessing and a curse.** If you imagine product knowledge gives you a license to educate the prospect, it's a curse.

3. **The real value of what you sell occurs when customers start using it.** It is the "future state" for them that drives their decision, so you need to be able to reach into the future for them and bring that into the present so they can visualize the benefits.

4. **Ask yourself the tough "So what?" questions before the customer does.** Your customers will be motivated by their reasons to buy, not your reasons to sell. After answering Pete's Question four or five times to yourself, you might start to approach the reason someone would want to buy from you.

CHAPTER 5

Cleaning Up

Or: A bootstrapper shows the difference between value and price

P at was faced with a classic bootstrapper choice. Should she sell on price to an unqualified prospect, or go the extra mile to find someone who would pay fair value for solving a real problem?

Tough jobs need tough tools, and in the world of machinery overhaul (Pat's chosen field), one of the toughest jobs was stripping off months, or even years, of accumulated dirt, debris and gunk. This process is sometimes called "degreasing," and it is not a task for the faint at heart.

The products used for this task are amongst the nastiest in the industrial world. If you mix one of them with any one of a hundred other products, they may well explode. If you should happen to spill them, you might literally have a toxic material incident on your hands. These products can give off highly toxic fumes and, of course, they tend to be very, very flammable.

Jeb worked in R&D. He was the product manager for a new line of deep cleaning degreasers. Their big advantage was that they were nowhere near as tricky and dangerous to handle as those of the competition. Based on initial trials, the new solvent was highly effective. What Jeb needed now was a real live customer to launch the product and, eventually, write a snazzy testimonial. Naturally, he went to Pat, the company's best salesperson, and asked her to bring someone on board. She was happy to discuss the project.

BUYING THE BUSINESS?

Jeb told Pat, "Senior management is right behind this launch. If you have to go in hard on price in order to win the business, rest assured you will get all the support you need."

"Hmm," Pat said. "So, you're telling me that if we lose money on this deal, the R&D department will make up the lost revenue to sales?"

That question hung in the air for a long moment.

"And while we are talking about money," Pat continued, "you do realize that in this company, salespeople are paid partly on profitability—not just on total sales value, right? So if I put together a deal that loses money, that will hit me personally. Will your department cover any shortfall I experience on that?"

Jeb actually hadn't thought things through that far. He was not normally closely involved in sales, but as product manager of the new line, he was determined to get the launch right with a great first customer.

"What I mean," Jeb said, "is that I know pricing will not be an issue. Trust me, you will get support for whatever you need to do."

"I appreciate that," Pat said. "So here is what I think we should do. I will go and meet with one of our biggest users, talk him through the idea and take his temperature on this. Once we get a feeling for his reaction, you and I can start talking about pricing. What do you think?"

TAKING THE TEMPERATURE

Jeb thought that made sense. So a few weeks later, Pat took a seat in the rather dark and grimy office of Hank, production manager of a company that did the overhaul and repair of major mobile machinery: earth movers, graders, off-road haulage trucks, and other equipment devoted to the toughest and dirtiest jobs in the world.

> *"I guess there is no way that it would make sense for anyone to move to next-generation product?"*

Pat had been dealing with Hank for over ten years and knew that he would be straight when they spoke. "We appreciate you giving us a first option on this," Hank said, "but to be honest, it doesn't seem like a priority for us right now. We have run trials on half a dozen great ideas to replace our solvent cleaners over the years, but right now it is not an issue. We have a well-trained crew, our health and safety people make sure we run a tight ship and the solvent we use is not a major cost item. Even if there were a savings, it is not a big enough gain to justify the effort in switching. If you bring this thing to market and find someone else to take the pain of being first to use it, then by all means walk right in here and we will talk. As it is, we are happy to avoid being on the bleeding edge of technology this time around."

The two knew each other well enough for Pat to recognize a "no" when it was as clear as this. "So, if cost and ease of use are not major factors, I guess there is no way that it would make sense for anyone to move to next-generation product?" asked Pat.

NEVER SAY "NEVER"

"Well, never say 'never,'" Hank said. "The real problem in using aggressive solvents nowadays is actually the storage. Virtually every other product we use is now suitable for standard warehousing, but solvents still need to have fire-retardant rooms in order to hold any reasonable volume. We rebuilt our storage facility about three years ago, though, so we are all covered on that front."

> *"Is there anyone we should take this to?"*

"Hank, I think you must know the business here better than anyone. Is there anyone we should take this to?"

Hank thought for a moment, and then said, "If I were you, I would take your idea over to Dean at Greenfield. Do you know him?"

"I met him once or twice," Pat answered, "but I wouldn't say that I know him. We've never done anything together. If you could give me an introduction, that would be great."

"I'll give him a call. Hope it works out for you."

"By the way, what makes you think that Dean might be open to this idea?"

"Well, they are opening a new line in his plant, and that means a lot of new building. Maybe it would make sense for them to start planning it with next-generation degreasers. Who knows?"

A few days later, Pat was standing in a partially constructed building with Dean. The new plant, Dean informed her, would handle heavy maintenance and overhaul of military equipment being brought home from an overseas facility where keeping things clean was almost impossible. Dean faced a huge challenge in terms of maintenance.

FIND THE PAIN, FIND THE BUDGET!

"Dean," Pat said, "I have no idea if this whole idea could even be relevant to you, but the people who have looked closely at this tell us that with this new solvent, there is much less requirement for extraction equipment, there looks to be a lot less of a problem in terms of handling and the product can be held in conventional storage facilities. But I don't want to assume that I know what is on your priority list right now."

> *"That's the idea. Why do you ask?"*

"To be frank," Dean said, "degreasers are not all that high on my list, but the cost of plant and machinery is. You're telling me that this stuff is basically non-flammable?"

"Yep. Our tech team has had it certified externally as being safe enough for standard storage. You can store it the same way you'd store containers of detergent."

"Hmm. So, no need for fire protection, huh?"

"That's the idea. Why do you ask?"

"If we can avoid having to build special storage units, then that will be a major headache solved. Before I even look at a trial I need to see your technical reports, and I also need to get an idea on pricing."

"That's not a problem," said Pat. "Can you let me have some idea of the volume you think you will be using?"

"We can give you a rough idea based on last year's use and our projections for the new line. Will that work?"

"If you get that to me, then I can come back to you within a few days with a pretty good estimate. It might be a bit more in terms of pricing than you are expecting, but let's see. Can we meet up at the end of next week to go over everything?"

Dean agreed. By the time Pat was back in the office, the estimated volumes from Dean had already arrived via email. She had tried to dig a little into the extra costs of the flammable material storage that Dean was considering, but he had been careful not to give too much away.

Jeb, the product manager, was overjoyed at the prospect of securing a launch customer in such a high-profile industry.

FACE TO FACE

Things seemed to be moving fast. Pat met with Dean a few days later.

"We don't want to spend all day bragging on about our product," she said. "I think that this is all about finding ways to cut down on the costs of secure storage and fume extraction. Is that still the case?" Pat knew that Dean had been through the technical side of the products carefully with Jeb over the phone and was satisfied with the performance levels.

"We're not ready to make a decision yet," said Dean. "But basically, yes, the win here for us is to strip out capital costs and probably ongoing disposal costs, too."

"You must have done some sort of analysis on the upside in terms of cost savings, correct?"

"If this all works out it will be worth it. Our accountant has built up a pretty solid business assessment."

"Do you mind if I ask what sort of number you used for pricing for the new product in your assessment?" asked Pat.

"You can ask, but that doesn't mean we are going to tell you. I think we are looking for you to make a proposal." Dean sat back in his chair, confident that he had played his trump card.

> *"You must have done some sort of analysis on the upside in terms of cost savings, correct?"*

Pat was now faced with one of the oldest dilemmas in sales: who should put a price on the table first? She noticed that Dean's body language had changed subtly. He seemed a little more tense, as though moving from the technical discussion onto money was a little outside his comfort zone.

TALKING NUMBERS

"Maybe I can talk you through how we normally work out pricing with other customers when we bring something like this to market. How does that sound?"

"Sure," Dean said.

"Typically all next-generation products in this market run to around a ten percent premium to the ones they replace. For the volumes you sent over to us, that would create a barrel price of between $125 and $155."

"That's a pretty broad range," said Dean, "but given the choice we would obviously go for $125. What's the driver here?"

"There are a number of moving parts here, such as minimum order size, payment terms, stock holding and a few other items. Also, we find that some people are focused on lowest unit price, while others care more about lowest total cost of use. We need to determine what works for you. A unit price of $155 brings a lot of add-on services from us that will probably mean that it works out cheaper for you in the long term."

"What sort of deal do you have with Hank? He recommended you, so I guess he must know your firm pretty well."

"That's a good question, Dean. Obviously we can't discuss

> *"Maybe I can talk you through how we normally work out pricing with other customers."*

the pricing we have with other companies, but I can tell you that Hank and his people expect a lot from us and rely a lot on our extra services. You should probably discuss that with him if you want to know more."

Dean became quiet as he began working out what tasks he might be able to get Pat's company to take off his desk. Eventually he looked up again. "What's the next step?"

"I was about to ask you the same question. You have a pretty good idea about the sort of problem we can help you resolve. You understand where we are in terms of pricing and budgets. What do you want to do next?"

"I suppose the next thing is to get our team together and set up this trial, right?"

By the way—the margin on the pricing Pat secured was more than enough to secure the seal of approval from her accounting department.

SANDLER TAKEAWAYS FOR BOOTSTRAPPERS

1. **Knowledge is power; assumptions can be deadly.** Having in-depth industry and product knowledge only has value if it helps you build the fastest way to a happy customer and a signed deal. How does your knowledge of the industry and product move you forward? How can you use what you know to understand the perspective of the prospective client?

2. **Control the pace, control the sale.** Professional selling is rarely a game for sprinters. Would you want to go to a doctor who rushed through the diagnosis? To earn your prospects'

trust, you need to demonstrate that you are in control of the process and that you care enough to understand both their pain and their perspective.

3. **Your price and their value are not the same thing.** Even in a pure commodity sale, the price you get and the value you generate are never the same. To get fair value for what you provide, you need to invest time and energy in uncovering why prospects would see you as the solution to their pain. Often, that pain is not something that was obvious at the outset.

4. **You never know too much about a problem.** Great salespeople are on a path of lifetime learning—and the greatest teachers in the world are usually their clients. Virtually every sale solves a slightly different pain. The more you understand about that pain, the greater the likelihood that you can resolve it profitably.

CHAPTER 6

The Great Prison Disaster

Or: An at-leaster learns that slick
presentations do not always lead to a sale

Carla thought it was the job of the marketing department to create the sales story, but she learned the hard way that what you think you are selling may not be what the prospect thinks he wants to buy.

Let's talk about one of the big confusions in business: the difference between sales and marketing.

You know that marketing is doing a good job when demand increases and salespeople find it a lot easier to close sales. From the perspective of a salesperson, you could even say that the role of marketing is to help salespeople close bigger deals faster. While that is not a complete definition, it is not too far from the truth.

The people who run the marking team know that their role

> *Sales is all about one-to-one storytelling.*

is about communicating their company's message to a wide audience. It is broad-brush communication. Salespeople need to be aligned to that message, but since they are the ones who are responsible for finding business, they own the responsibility to tell that story in a way that resonates with specific customers. Sales is all about one-to-one storytelling. The more you sound like you are reading from a corporate brochure, the less you sound like you are telling a story that matters to the person in front of you.

As an example, let's look at the events around the "Great Prison Disaster." It is a story that anyone in sales may well recognize from his own career.

A GOOD START

The Great Prison Disaster started harmlessly enough. In fact it started positively. It happened during the early years of the environmental revolution, when industry started taking all sorts of toxic nastiness out of products and replacing them with what is now called "green technology." Carla worked in a firm dedicated to introducing cutting-edge, environmentally friendly products into the building maintenance market. Carla, and the rest of the sales team, was called down to the head office to see a new product launch—a new range of paints for high-traffic areas. The presentation was a hit. Everyone at the launch agreed the products were great, not just because the marketing people said they were great, but because they had proof of it.

The marketing people wanted to arm the sales force with as much ammunition as they could and had put together a great list of things these new paints could do. The new paint was:

- Environmentally friendly and less smelly.
- Faster drying.
- Tougher and longer lasting.

Carla took a lot of notes, got a copy of the presentation material and studied up on the technology side to make sure that she could cover any questions.

One of the biggest customers in Carla's territory was the local prison system, which had a lot of wall space in its buildings that needed to be painted and a lot of people living there who did not seem to care too much about keeping their environment neat and tidy.

Carla called the head of maintenance for the biggest prison in the area and offered to do a free seminar for the maintenance supervisors. As a sweetener, she offered free T-shirts from the new product launch as well as a case of cola to get them in the room.

SLICK PRESENTATION

Carla's presentation was good; she had practiced for hours and she knew all her facts, so she was ready to rock and roll when the room began to fill up with half a dozen grizzled maintenance supervisors. She took a deep breath, visualized success and launched into her presentation. It was a nightmare.

Having snatched the T-shirts and grabbed the drinks, the supervisors sat down and played "rattle the salesperson" for the next hour. Nothing Carla said had the slightest impact. Her "faster drying" point earned a witty response along the lines that their customers were not going anywhere, so what was the hurry? Being "longer lasting" didn't win any friends either, as apparently

> *"It has nothing to do with their job,
> so why should they care?"*

prisons "were not meant to be pretty." Being environmentally friendly brought open laughter.

Carla's collection of maintenance supervisors trooped out just before her presentation finished convinced of two things. First, that Carla was an idiot, and second, that nothing she had said was even slightly relevant to them.

Fortunately the maintenance manager who had set the meeting up took some pity.

"None of these people give a hoot if your stuff is green, stays pretty, and dries faster," he said. "It has nothing to do with their job, so why should they care?"

CARING A BIT

Fortunately, this one person did care a bit—just enough to turn her entire marketing presentation upside down.

"Look, Carla, when you see a prison, you see a big building full of bad guys. When we see a prison, we see how many people can be kept in there every year. We call it 'cell nights.' If your stuff dries faster, we can get the cells back into use faster, so more cell nights per year. Do you see?"

Carla saw.

"If the stuff really does last longer, it might be that we don't have to repaint as often so we can extend the maintenance cycle—saving a lot of money. Get it?"

Carla got it.

"The last thing is that we hate paperwork in this business. When we have to get rid of dangerous waste, we need to fill in a lot of forms. If your stuff is so green, then we probably don't need special waste disposal and that means less paperwork for us. Make sense?"

It did.

A few weeks after her crushing at the seminar, Carla called every one of those supervisors with her new approach. "Hi, this is Carla—yes, the 'T-shirt with a drink' lady. I have been working with another prison, and we have found a way to increase cell nights, extend maintenance cycles and get rid of a ton of paperwork. Are any of those things relevant to you?"

> **"Are any of those things relevant to you?"**

It took her a year, but that prison service became one of her company's best customers—and, to everyone's surprise, was at the cutting-edge of green technology.

SANDLER TAKEAWAYS FOR BOOTSTRAPPERS

1. **Selling is a play, performed by psychologists.** Salespeople do have a script they want to work with, and prospects probably have a plot they want to see played out. What you have to do is to play out that storyline but treat the whole experience as though you are a psychologist, studying the other players and improvising your lines to match.

2. **Comfort zones can be performance traps.** Once you master a subject, it is great to share what you know. Giving a presentation can be nerve-wracking, but running through a prepared script can keep you in your comfort zone. Probably the best presentation in sales is the one you never give. Having all that preparation complete gives you an armory of things to use. Using that armory without thought may be comfortable, but remember the focus in sales is on what the prospect says, not what you say.

3. **If marketing could solve the sales problem, they wouldn't need salespeople.** Features and benefits tell you what you are selling, but if you can't get to the bottom of the actual

problems you solve or the value you create, then you are doing less than half the job.

4. **Business buyers are just consumers in a business environment.** People buy everything, even the most complex products in the world, because they believe that their own lives will be somehow better after they buy that thing. Selling quarter-inch holes instead of quarter-inch drills is a good start, but understanding what the hole will do for the customer is where real sales and real value lie.

CHAPTER 7

Best News in the World

Or: A bootstrapper discovers the best prospect is the client right in front of you

It feels great to find a new client, but that's not all there is to selling. Robert was justifiably proud when he made a new sale, but he also learned to exercise the everyday bravery that turned a sale into a relationship.

"Hi, Robert, this is Ed. Look, I'm sorry it has taken me so long to get back to you. You know what this place is like when it comes to administration. Anyway, the reason I am calling is to tell you some good news. The COO met with the finance people this morning, and they made the final decision. We are good to go with your proposal, and we need you to come in as soon as possible to sign some paperwork and finalize the start date and delivery schedule."

There are few phone calls in a salesperson's career that feel bet-

> *"I don't need to tell you how happy*
> *we are to be selected."*

ter than this. Robert had been fighting long and hard in a very competitive bid to supply one of the country's major engineering companies with a high-precision fluid control system. The system delivered tightly controlled amounts of chemical solution into testing vessels at high speed: precision was critical, as was dependability. It had taken a lot of support from other people in Robert's team to land this deal, and now he had the privilege of telling everyone involved that they had won. But before that, he needed to go through the final steps in closing the deal.

END OF THE SALE?

"Ed, I don't need to tell you how happy we are to be selected as your partner. People on both sides put a lot of effort into this, and we are grateful for the support your team gave us. I am traveling right now, but I can be in your office Friday morning to handle the paperwork and nail down dates and details. Does that work for you?"

It worked for Ed, and they spent a few minutes in the relaxed conversation that tends to come after a major deal is agreed.

As soon as he said goodbye to Ed, Robert bought himself a coffee, found a comfortable seat, and began calling his team to share the good news—and also, to be honest, to enjoy the wave of congratulations that flowed his way. His boss was happy, his boss's boss was happy, and he had a very cheerful call with his head of production, who was happy he could start his planning a few days early and not have the contract land on his desk without warning as had happened in the past.

A small celebration for the team was suggested by his divisional VP. It might only be a pizza and bowling night, but Robert knew that he would be the man of the moment.

It was only when he spoke with Colin, his CFO, that the glow began to wear off the day.

THE BEGINNING OF THE NEXT STEP

"We've done some work for these guys before," said Colin, "but only on a small-scale basis. For us to supply on this contract, we need to revise their customer account details. We'll be shipping some high-value systems to them, so the credit control team will need to run their credit worthiness checks."

Robert's day suddenly got cloudier. Obviously, the credit control people had a job to do—an important job—but sometimes he felt that they were more interested in keeping their filing up-to-date than focusing on the things that actually brought in the money and kept the company afloat.

"You should check in with Ann," said Colin. "I know you will want to see this thing moving quite quickly, so you'd better talk to the head honcho."

Despite his many years of senior sales and his ability to hold his own with C-level executives from his clients, Robert's blood ran a little colder at the very mention of Ann's name. She knew her job unbelievably well, she had never been known to make a mistake and her team was devoted to her. Almost no one ever left her department, and when they did it tended to be for internal promotion. Unfortunately, Ann was not known for her interpersonal skills. If something needed to be said, she tended to just say it. She knew that money was a difficult subject for a lot people to discuss, so she had learned long ago that the best thing to do was put the issue right out on the table. She took the same direct approach with all business matters.

NOTHING PERSONAL

With Ann involved, there was no point in ducking the issue of credit control. Robert called her, gave a brief summary of the new contract and set a time to meet for later that week—he wanted to have this conversation face-to-face. It was important to impress on Ann the need to be diplomatic with such an important new client.

Before facing Ann, Robert gathered every scrap of documentation he could find on this contract and the financial side of the deal. He also found an organizational chart of the client to show who was who. With any luck, he might be able to run the actual conversations with the client himself and keep Ann in the background.

But Ann was way ahead of him. "I was speaking to our new client Ed yesterday about the steps we need to take to review their credit worthiness for this contract." The very idea of this conversation filled Robert with horror, but Ann seemed not to notice the change in his expression.

"There is a bit of work to do here," she continued. "If they move at the speed you propose in the contract, we will have a lot of outstanding invoices with them right at the end of our fiscal year. That's something we like to avoid, but I guess it is too late to make any changes now."

> *"You could make sure that you sell
> more to our existing customers."*

"So, you already spoke with Ed?" asked Robert.

"We need to get some credit references to upgrade his account with us. To be honest, it is a bit of a pain coming right now. This is the equivalent of creating a new account, and it has come at a very busy time."

Robert was still thinking of ways in which he could lessen the impact of Ann and her team of number crunchers talking to Ed and his team. "Is there something I can do to help?" he asked hopefully.

Ann paused for a moment, thinking. "Yes, there is actually. It would save a ton of money for the firm."

"Really?" said Robert, genuinely surprised.

"You could make sure that you sell more to our existing customers, rather than doing all these one-at-a-time deals. I don't suppose you give it any thought, but it costs the equivalent of $25,000 worth of administration time and external checks to open a major new credit account, and this will be more or less the same effort."

Robert was stunned. He had closed a sizeable deal with the industry leader, a major strategic target for his firm, and the only comment Ann had was she would have preferred him to sell to an existing client.

DID I HEAR THAT RIGHT?

Robert left the meeting with Ann with a much less rosy view of the world than he had entered it with—in fact he could barely believe what she had said.

Later that day, he was sitting at lunch with his boss Margaret, and he relayed the conversation he had had with Ann to her. Much to his surprise and disappointment, Margaret immediately sided with Ann.

"Yup, account management is a major drain on that team right now," said Margaret. "They want to be focusing on much more important projects, but they keep getting bogged down in sales-related issues. New accounts take a ton of resources and are our highest risk."

> *"Selling to an existing customer is much, much more profitable than cracking a new one."*

"So, the company would prefer that we did not win business with new clients, but kept calling on the ones we have?"

"Robert, our three top priorities are: close the business, close the business, and close the business. Maybe, number four might be to keep in mind that selling to an existing customer is much, much more profitable than cracking a new one. Ann might be a bit tough on the outside sometimes, but you will never meet anyone more dedicated to making this company successful. She deserves every ounce of the respect she gets from the leadership team. If I were an ambitious salesperson, I would listen carefully to any advice she took the time to give me."

PAUSE FOR THOUGHT

One of the greatest gifts a person can have in business is to be able to recognize good advice when it is offered. The words of both Ann and Margaret ran through Robert's head frequently in the run-up to his contract finalization meeting with Ed. If Robert's firm wanted to do more business with existing clients, then there was no better place to start than with their newest one.

Robert prepared well for his meeting. All the documents were in order, the project plan had no real changes, and there were no last-minute tricks on Ed's side to try and squeeze a little extra on the pricing, Ed was even complimentary about his conversations with Ann over credit control.

Everything in Robert's mind was telling him to keep smiling, keep the customer happy, take the contract, and head out for beer and pizza to celebrate with the guys. But strangely, over the past few days he had developed an ambition to meet up with Ann sometime in the future and say to her, "Ann, I listened to what you said about selling more to our existing clients, and this is what I have done about it."

Until he spoke with Ann, he thought his job was to make the sale. But now that he had started thinking like a bootstrapper, he saw his responsibility as focusing on the whole business. This sale was just one step of his mission. As he watched Ed sign the contract, he mustered up his strength and spoke.

"Ed," he said, "it is great to be working with you on this. You know we will deliver for you."

"Thanks, Robert," Ed said. "We have every confidence."

> *"Are there any other areas of your company that might benefit from the sort of services we are providing you and your team?"*

"Good. We hope this contract is the start of a strong relationship between our companies. Do you mind if I ask if there are any other areas of your company that might benefit from the sort of services we are providing you and your team?"

Ed's brow furrowed for a moment. "I'll tell you what we could do," he said. "We are having a two-day off-site meeting with myself and all the other heads of research and development. We have been talking about bringing in external suppliers to showcase studies of how joint projects could be run. I think this project would make a good study for us to discuss. You'll meet all the other R&D leaders there, and if you want to follow up with them you can. How does that sound?"

Robert left the meeting holding not only a signed contract but almost certainly the best prospecting opportunity he had had in his career. More than that, he knew that in this meeting, he had gone the extra mile.

SANDLER TAKEAWAYS FOR BOOTSTRAPPERS

1. **Develop a "prospecting awareness."** One of the greatest challenges in sales is finding new prospects. It is time-consuming and can be a heartbreaking experience. Salespeople need to develop a constant awareness of where the next prospective deal might come from, and often the best opportunities are right in front of them in their existing client base. When you have resolved a pain with a client, isn't that the ideal time to find out what else you can do for him and his organization?

2. **The purpose of selling is taking money to the bank.** For a lot of people, selling can be a great way to boost their ego. Getting things done, making a difference, and solving problems for people are all highly laudable, but the real goal of selling is to generate income. When you sell, you need to leave your ego in the car and focus on maximizing the revenue stream.

3. **The difference between a good sale and a great sale is probably less than five percent extra sales effort.** Five seconds of everyday bravery is often the magic difference between adequate and excellent performance. In virtually every sales situation, there is a decision to be made—a choice between two paths. We at Sandler often call this "Wimp Junction"—should you take the easy road, or the tougher, more professional route? Nine times out of ten, the tougher road is the one to greater sales performance.

4. **The signed contract is not the end—it is the start of the next phase of your relationship.** You aren't just selling products or services; you are selling a relationship, a future state for your clients. Far too often, salespeople who are the prospect's hero during the sales phase disappoint the client by disappearing in a puff of smoke the minute the contract is signed.

CHAPTER 8

Learning from Complexity the Hard Way

Or: An at-leaster discovers the difference
between a buddy and a business relationship

While it is true that people like to buy from those with whom they find it easy to communicate—an idea reinforced daily when colleagues tell us, "This is a relationship business"—there are more factors at play. Bob invested a lot of time and effort in building what he thought were great business relationships, but he found out the hard way that people also buy from those who bring value to them.

There is nothing wrong with relationship building as long as you do not let that become your only sales approach. Being friendly is not selling, especially when the sale is complex and the customer has several decision makers.

Selling in the scotch whisky business was a challenging experience for Bob. It was the second role in his sales career, and the

> *People like to buy from those with whom*
> *they find it easy to communicate.*

industry was fairly "old school." All contracts were renegotiated annually, and competition was fierce since the packaging Bob's firm sold was nearly always sourced from several suppliers. It kept suppliers hungry, and it kept life interesting.

Fortunately for Bob something had clicked with the biggest of his new clients when he joined the business; he got on really well with their product development team, their operations people were open to new ideas and always willing to share their agendas in terms of business improvement, and their marketing people seemed more than keen to find out what proactive suppliers like Bob's were able to do. It was sales-guy heaven, and Bob was one of the gang on the inside.

BUDDY-BUDDY

There were times when Bob's buddy-buddy relationship with his customer was viewed quite critically by his own company. Sometimes Bob appeared to be too much the "customer's champion" during internal discussions about pricing and cost sharing. "Whose side are you on?" was an accusing question thrown at him more than once. Having mulled it over for a while, he worked out a believable response: "I'm on the side of the business relationship." He would say this smugly and use it as his basis for spending ever more time hanging out with his pals inside the client's company.

The relationship deepened. Bob and his champions even shared a common enemy—the client's own purchasing department. In almost every meeting Bob had with his contacts, there would be a great flow of energy with new ideas coming thick and fast. Then somebody would throw a wet blanket over the whole thing by mentioning that they would need to get the "purchasing police" involved. Every joint project seemed to grind to a halt over such fun and productive subjects as cost-benefit analysis, strategic purchasing policies, vendor approval ratings, and the ever-popular business case presentation. Every question they answered created two more questions straight back, more paperwork, more justification, and more delay.

> *Every question they answered created*
> *two more questions straight back.*

Bob would sit long into the evening with his counterparts from the customer side dreaming up ways to try and circumvent the evil grasp of the purchasing police, which earned them the new nickname of "progress prevention department." More than once Bob went to the customer's senior management to get their blessing for a clever shortcut that cut out procurement, and often he won.

Then the annual contract negotiations came around.

NEGOTIATION

With so much of this customer's products being sourced from multiple suppliers, Bob's firm always knew that they had to fight their corner. Bob and his manager put together a great negotiation pack. They worked out their opening stance, what they realistically expected to get, and what their true "walk away" pricing was. Bob spent a long, long time creating a truly marvelous 45-slide presentation, modestly boasting about his firm's tremendous contribution to the client's business with its agile and innovative product development process. Bob's management was pleased, and he became a little bit of a star internally with his snappy pitch. Other members of the sales team were told to "copy Bob's approach," making him less than popular with some of his colleagues as well.

The client team sat patiently through the contract proposal from Bob's firm, dozed quietly through his slide presentation, and told Bob they would respond to all suppliers in due course.

When the client team eventually made their responses to Bob's proposal, his firm's share of their business had been reduced by nearly 30 percent—a seven-figure sum in cash terms.

> *It is the whole relationship that matters.*

Bob's bosses were not happy. He was less of a star all of a sudden.

His manager told him to set up a meeting between his CEO and their CEO to find out what had gone so horribly wrong. The meeting went a bit like this:

Bob's CEO: Our people worked hard with your people all year, and I thought we had done some good things. We were a bit surprised when you took 30 percent of our business away and gave it to our competitors.

Client's CEO: Yes, I can well imagine that was an unpleasant piece of news.

Bob's CEO: Very unpleasant, and we are a bit confused. Perhaps you could tell us what caused you to make such a big decision?

Client's CEO: It turns out that some members of our leadership team think that your company can't be trusted.

Bob's CEO: Can't be trusted? What do you mean by that, if you don't mind my asking?

Client's CEO: From the feedback we had during our internal contract review, it seems that your team spends a lot of time finding creative ways to circumvent our strategic purchasing policies, our vendor approval-rating system and our process for reviewing business cases. We hear that some of your people almost gang up with some of our people to create clever workarounds in order to avoid working with our Purchasing Department. We don't like suppliers playing clever games with our internal processes. That's why we reduced your business with us.

WHERE ARE ALL MY FRIENDS?

Bob wasn't fired, but sacking him would not have been a surprising course of action. The worst blow came when Bob told his good friends within the customer's company about how shocking the purchasing leader's behavior had been with him and his firm. What was their response? "Well, he was just doing his job, I suppose."

No matter how close the personal bonds seem to be with your strongest allies at a client's company, it is the whole relationship that matters. That means having a solid and cold perspective on who drives the buying decisions. Customers may ask you along to their social events, but there is no point in being invited to the barbecue if you are not invited to the board room, too.

SANDLER TAKEAWAYS FOR BOOTSTRAPPERS

1. **It's not about making friends.** It is so very easy to confuse personal friendships with effective business relationships, and that confusion can be deadly. Keeping your distance is one of

the most important—and one of the most forgotten—rules in sales relationships.

2. **Set your own course.** Your company will have a set of things it wants to achieve in its client relationships. Your customer will also have a set of objectives that he wants, and—surprise, surprise—they may not be an exact match. Nobody has a bigger stake than you when it comes to creating a path that both firms can accept.

3. **Map out the people side of the buyer.** There are two sides to complex purchasing processes (the human and the organizational), and there are dozens of great books about complex strategic sales planning, but the simplest and best way is to grab a blank sheet of paper and write at the top: "People inside the customer's company who can influence the decision to buy from me." The next smart thing to do is to show it to someone within your company who can help fill it in and brainstorm good ideas on servicing them. If you are lucky, you might have an ally within the customer's company. If you do and you feel comfortable talking to him, show him your piece of paper, too. Once you do all of that, you will have one of the best account plans you will ever see—with nary a slide presentation in sight.

CHAPTER 9

Across the Lawn and Into the Wilderness

Or: A bootstrapper learns a lot from some dumb questions

S alespeople are sometimes convinced they need to spend their sales time and effort in the world of complexity. In fact, bootstrapper Ivana knew that meaningful sales development, even with the most complex clients, often needs the help of some dumb questions.

"I need to ask a really dumb question," she said to her client representatives. "Do you mind if I ask exactly where a decision like this gets made?"

Ivana was talking to the head of operations and the VP of procurement for one of her company's best clients, and she was putting together a proposal for a new integrated logistics system that would manage all national bulk deliveries. It was a massive deal: minimum five-year duration; purchase of a whole fleet of both trucks and trailers; a major software implementation; and a total headcount into the hundreds.

They had worked with this client for several years, but so far only on a regional basis. If this proposal went through, it would make this client their number one international logistics partner.

> *"I need to ask you a really dumb question."*

The client, a major retailer, was famous for its near obsession with controlling every detail of the operation centrally. Retail can be a very tight margin business, and it is often the one with the best control on the small stuff that produces the profits.

RIGHT THERE IN TOWN

Everything was done right there, in the town where the company had been formed generations ago. Every pricing decision, every product launch and every contract was decided in the complex of buildings that the company had built, known to everyone as "the campus."

The reason for Ivana's dumb question was that there was a flip side to the client's obsession with control; they hated to be controlled by anyone else, and their standard answer to any supplier who pushed them was, "We'll get back to you."

In practice, this meant that suppliers would be left dangling, often for months, waiting for the client to make a decision. Not surprisingly, it made forecasting a nightmare, as salespeople had no idea when a contract might be placed.

Ivana had been burned this way before with this client. Two

years prior, she had negotiated a good-sized deal for her firm to take over a client's onsite logistics: forklift trucks, scanning systems and staffing for one of the central distribution hubs. Everything had been agreed, emails had even been sent confirming their selection and then—nothing. For over four months there was virtual silence. Every question from Ivana and her company was greeted with a sympathetic shrug and the endlessly repeated response, "It's in the system. Leave it with us. We'll get back to you."

YOU CAN'T BEAT THE SYSTEM

Whatever "the system" was, it wasn't fast. The long delay became a constant feature of her discussions with her own head office. Several senior people made the trip to the client's offices to press for progress. Every one came back with the same message: "It's in the system."

One Friday afternoon an email popped up in Ivanna's inbox with the signed purchase order. Ivana called her boss, and then went out and had a great Friday night. But in reality, her main emotion was relief rather than triumph. It turned out that the proposal had been stuck on the desk of a project leader who had been tasked with making sure all distribution centers used the same order checking process. He wasn't going to sign off on Ivana's proposal until his project team finished their review.

This time, Ivana thought, things would be different. She bought a whiteboard and put it on the wall of her home office. She called it her "war board."

In the top left-hand corner of the board, she wrote the word, "Who."

Having been ambushed by some unseen project manager once before, she was definitely not going to let that happen again. As the new deal began to look more and more likely, she began asking the question, "Do you mind if I ask, who else might be involved in this decision?" She wanted to track down every decision maker and every possible influencer that she could. When that question apparently uncovered the names of all the people, including project managers, who would need to approve a deal like hers, she switched up another gear.

WHO ELSE?

"Could you help me understand who would be impacted by this move if it goes ahead?" With those answers, Ivana would work to find a host of other people who were not in the actual decision process but could potentially throw a wrench in the works somewhere down the line.

She always sought permission from the procurement people before talking to anyone, but gradually she worked her way through almost every stakeholder and influencer she could find. She got their thoughts, feedback and concerns. As much as possible, she made sure that everyone's concerns were covered in the proposal and the support documentation.

This deal was the biggest item in the company's pipeline. Not surprisingly, it had garnered plenty of attention. Ivana took a photo of her war board and showed it to her boss Tony, the EVP for business development.

> *"Who would be impacted by this move if it goes ahead?"*

"I don't think I have ever seen a better plan for dealing with the people side of a buying decision," he said when he saw the image. "It's a great start."

"When you say 'start,' it gives me the feeling that you think there is a lot more still to do," responded Ivana.

"Obviously, the human side is critical, but from what you tell me these guys are pretty process driven, too. What do all these people need to see in terms of checkboxes, business cases and impact analyses?"

"I think I have that. I spoke to everyone on this war board."

"Great," said Tony. "Why not write it up? We can then sit down together and talk through it."

AFTER THE "WHO," THE "WHAT"

Ivana was surprised by what she learned when she started asking around. The people within the client's organization spoke a different language. Almost everyone needed some sort of specific document or prior approval before signing off themselves. Most were happy that Ivana showed an interest in lightening their load, and she gained a huge amount of information she could use to help move the decision process through the system faster. She began compiling a file full of quality audits, staff training plans, risk assessments and procedures that people wanted to see before they could make an informed decision and give their approval to Ivana's project.

As she worked through this list of things that people needed—she called it her "What" list—she also realized that this was not just a bunch of data that people needed; there was a fair amount of process involved, too. It seemed that "How" the people used the data was also critical. For example, insurance liability could not be discussed in a meaningful way until staff training had been understood, and that needed a good understanding of how people were trained.

By now, Ivana's whiteboard was getting pretty full. The "Who," "What," and "How" information was getting tough to handle, but it was telling a strong story.

COMPELLING EVENT?

"There is only the big one still to go," said Ivana during one of her regular sales reviews with Tony. "That is, 'When?' All we ever hear is that they want this done for the start of next year, but so far I have never heard of anything particularly bad that will happen if they miss that date."

> ### "So there is no compelling event?"

"So there is no compelling event?" asked Tony.

"Right. First, there isn't any hard date or event that is driving this deal. Second, these guys hate the idea of a 'compelling event.' They do not like to see themselves as being compelled by anything external."

"And so our plan is...?"

"To identify and eliminate every obstacle we can find to them hitting their target date."

"OK," said Tony. "That sounds like the best plan we have. Is there anything missing from your war board questions?"

"Only one, but it seems pretty dumb. There is the 'where' question. We know that every decision in the company is made at the campus, but I guess it will take me a 10-second investment of time to ask that dumb question. Who knows? We might get something new."

So a few weeks later, Ivana found herself in a room with some of the key decision makers from the client. She took a deep breath and went for it.

"I need to ask you a dumb question. Do you mind if I ask exactly where a decision like this gets made?"

OVER THE LAWN

"Right here on campus," said the head of procurement.

"So this is an operational decision made in this building?" asked Ivana.

"Absolutely, the operations leadership team will make the decision. Of course, once this is done it goes over the lawn."

In all the years that Ivana had worked with the client she had never heard the phrase "over the lawn" before. It sent a small chill along her spine.

"When you say 'over the lawn,' what you mean?"

"Well, this project has capital implications. We will be co-funding a lot of new hardware, so there are some liability and treasury implications. Our treasury team works from the small building on the other side of the lawn. Since this deal looks like it may be over $25 million, our treasury team needs to give it a rubber stamp. It is purely a formality though."

> *"Sorry to ask such a dumb question."*

"And under $25 million in capital value? What happens then?"

"Projects under that amount are purely operational. Treasury is not involved."

"That is really interesting to know. I am grateful for the information. Sorry to ask such a dumb question."

As soon as she was outside the building she called Tony.

"Tony, right now our year-one proposal is looking like just over $26.5 million. I think we need to look at restructuring the numbers to make sure our first year comes in under 25."

NO SUCH THING AS A FORMALITY

It was a short call. Both she and Tony were experienced enough to know that there was no such thing as a team of financial analysts going through a review that was "purely a formality." If another group of decision influencers were going to be involved, particularly a group with whom they had no relationship, it could only mean delay—and probably an extended period of reselling.

Before submission, the proposal was restructured to bring the first year in under the $25 million benchmark. For the first time in their history with the client, a deal was signed right on time.

SANDLER TAKEAWAYS FOR BOOTSTRAPPERS

1. **Investing in uncovering the decision-making process nearly always pays dividends.** In a first-time sale to a new client the value is easy to see, but far too often familiarity with existing customers blinds a sales team to the fact that every sale is a new potential phase in the relationship. Of all the times I have ever asked the question, "Do you mind if I ask how your organization normally makes this kind of decision?" I have almost always received an answer that taught me something about my client I didn't know.

2. **Our prospect might need our help.** Often the process is of real value to the prospect, but they may not have planned out the internal approval pathway for the deal they are championing. It is worth remembering that prospects are likely to have a lot less experience at buying your solutions than you do at selling them.

3. **Dummy up on the questions.** "Dummy questions," those basic questions that new guys ask when they first join the company, can be incredibly valuable. Interestingly, they are also the types of big, basic questions that you hear CEOs ask. The

danger zone comes in the middle of a career when it's easy to think you know a bit more than you actually do—and you fall into the comfort zone of technical talk.

4. **Don't reinvent the wheel.** You have processes that allow you to free your mind for more important things, like actually listening to prospects. If you know you need to get the answers to *who, what, where, when* and *how* (sometimes even *why*), then you can prepare for that conversation with an easy checklist. Always listen to your instinct, but use the process to work out where you are and where the gaps in your knowledge lie.

CHAPTER 10

Not Waving but Drowning

Or: Lack of product knowledge saves an at-leaster
from running in a race she could never win

Very often the markets that seem to be the most simple are in fact the most complex. Some markets are so insular that it's impossible to break into them from outside. Sara had been a classic "features, advantages and benefits" salesperson for years until she found herself in an industry where she could not even get up to walking speed with her clients.

Never had it been harder to gain knowledge of a product range than the day Sara looked down at a massive table of swatches that made up the current year's waterproof fabrics she would sell in her new job. The product was quite rightly surrounded by a mountain of intellectual protection to keep it safe and secure. Even during her training, there were labs and equipment that Sara was not allowed to see.

What she was allowed to see was a lot of fabrics that all made exactly the same claim—they were waterproof. They also had invisible holes so that when you sweated the moisture could escape, and they all seemed built to last forever.

One of the biggest problems of selling such an intricate product line was that the industry was populated by thoroughly knowledgeable people who had worked in the business their entire careers. What's more, it seemed to Sara that their spare-time activities revolved around leaping about in the great outdoors using clothing made of the fabric her firm produced.

KNOWING THE PRODUCT

Sara's company gave her all the time in the world to get up to speed on their products. The company sent her to labs and production sites. She met technical specialists who were only too happy to educate her. She dedicated time to staring at the product range. But, to be honest, the task was so large and the subject so very dull (to her) that after several weeks of training she had absorbed nothing beyond the initial information she'd gained in the first few days.

The firm's PhDs were physically unable to talk at the level of Sara's ignorance. Every person she met was vastly more qualified than she was at understanding her company's mission and products.

> In the past, she had relied on killer product knowledge.

Since the rest of Sara's working world looked like they were 15 years ahead of her, she was in way over her head. The idea of trying to sell to customers who knew much more than she did about her own product was frankly terrifying. In the past, she had relied on killer product knowledge to solve a customer's problems, but this was another game all together.

If you can't talk about the trees, talk about the forest. Sara managed to fake her way through her first meetings by talking about industry trends and big news she had read in trade magazines. Eventually, though, there was nowhere to hide. The chief designer of her biggest customer, Chris, wanted to see what was new and exciting in that year's collection. Sara did her best to study what had changed in her firm's product range since the prior year and headed off to her date with imminent disaster.

THE SHOCK OF TELLING THE TRUTH

At the client's offices, Sara unloaded her bulky sample books in the meeting room.

"Thanks for coming down, Sara," said Chris. "Let's have a look at what you have for us for next year."

Apart from folders full of identical fabric swatches, the only tool Sara had was the list of the prior year's orders. Since there was no way that she could fake it, she fell back on the strongest tool in any salesperson's toolbox—she told the truth.

> *"We would love to hear your ideas on how that would work."*

"Chris," Sara said, "this is a list of all the things your firm bought from us last year. How about we go through all these new fabrics, and you tell me how they might sit with your ideas for next year? If you want to swap out one of last year's products for one of these new ones, we would love to know why. If we have something in the new fabrics that you think could help you do something brand new, then we would love to hear your ideas on how that would work, too."

That sounded like a workable plan to Chris. He then spent the rest of the day teaching Sara why his firm was willing to buy her firm's very expensive fabrics and why one piece of cloth was of greater interest than another. Sara took a lot of notes.

WHY WOULD YOU WANT TO BUY THAT?

If Chris spent a lot of time with a particular sample, Sara would ask him why it was so interesting and what about it could work for him. Similarly, when he skipped over one, she would ask him why. At the end of the day Sara had a list of fabrics that Chris wanted larger samples of and a lot of detailed notes. For every sample that he took a real interest in, Sara would get him to tell her what he would use it for, why the existing range did not cover that need and what the potential impact would be for him.

Back at the office, Sara sent a long email covering every comment Chris had made to her technical people.

> *The technical talk crowded out the possibility of having meaningful business discussions.*

A week or so later, Sara's boss said that their technical team had told him that her notes from that meeting were the best feedback they had ever received from a salesperson. Sara's colleagues, who were much more knowledgeable than she was now or would probably ever be, tended to pass on only a few highlights from their customer meetings. There was so much shared knowledge between sales and technology that feedback seemed to be redundant.

It turned out that in a business environment populated by industry experts, the technical talk crowded out the possibility of having meaningful business discussions. Sara's lack of product or industry knowledge had forced her to work outside her normal comfort zone and instead spend the meeting talking about her customer's business needs, not those of her company.

SANDLER TAKEAWAYS FOR BOOTSTRAPPERS

1. **Shocking, disarming honesty.** Few tools in sales are as convincing as openness. Far too often salespeople fall into the trap of believing that sales is a contest between themselves and their prospects; confrontation is almost expected. Using honesty can break that negative pattern to establish a real bond and basis for mutual respect.

2. **Knowledge is power; information rarely is.** Almost everything you know about your product and market can be found by an intelligent client online within minutes. A lot of salespeople love to pick up bits of jargon and flaunt them in the hope this will increase their credibility. But the risk is huge. The value you create when in a sales situation is your ability to bring two sets of people together in a way that benefits them both.

3. **Selling is all about the money.** A lot of people within an organization sell, but only salespeople sell exclusively. The purpose of meeting people is to sell things to them, not to earn praise or appreciation for your stunning technical knowledge.

4. **Insatiable curiosity.** Almost anyone who sells has a competitor. Almost everything that people buy has an alternative that could replace it. If there is a single prime directive that anyone in sales should adopt, it is to develop a deep curiosity about why people might choose to work with you rather than with somebody else.

CHAPTER 11

Fun

Or: How a bootstrapper learned to have fun and make money at the same time

Most people spend a large part of their waking lives at work. For better or worse, they also spend a lot of their non-working hours thinking about work. So the influence of work on people's lives is critical. If work behavior was the same as home behavior, this might not be much of an issue. But the reality for most people is that work requires a "work face." You have to switch on a professional personality, leaving some parts of who you are at home. Of course there is a good reason for this—work is serious. It needs dedicated, professional focus and energy, using genuine knowledge and skills. It is not a place where many can afford to mess around too much. But it is also part of the human condition, where people working together make sales and purchasing decisions that can have a big impact on the lives of others.

Josh often found it hard to separate his "work" self from his "real" self. His attitude was pretty much the same on Sunday mornings when he was walking his dog and reading the Sunday paper as it was on Monday morning when he was up to his neck in complex sales issues and tough negotiations. Sometimes it seemed to his bosses that he was a little too laid back, and more than once he had been accused of not being "engaged" enough in his job. In reality, it was that he would forget to leave the relaxed, funny side of himself back home every morning. He brought all of himself to work.

> *Josh often found it hard to separate his "work" self from his "real" self.*

Despite the fact that Josh was a thoroughly modern sales professional, he had chosen to work in one of the oldest industries in the world. Josh's company built trains. Trains helped create the modern world. Despite having been around for almost 200 years, trains are still an important part of the infrastructure around the world. Josh was deeply involved in a project to provide trains for one of the new high-speed rail systems that was, amazingly enough, helping to replace airline transport for shorter journeys.

SLOW DOWN

The bad news was that Josh's project had stopped moving. Everyone had moved a bit too fast in the beginning, leaving a lot of assumptions untested and quite a few decisions hanging in the wind. To get to the next stage, a surprising number of tough decisions had to be made—decisions that meant one side or the other might have to pay out money.

Because of the feedback Josh had received that he put his best "office" face on when he met the client, he never betrayed any emotion. He kept his Sunday morning self under wraps.

The tougher the situation got between his firm and the client's team, the more "professional" everybody seemed to get—and the more professional everyone got, the less things seemed to be moving. Everyone dug themselves into solid positions to defend their side's interests and just as effectively make sure that nothing practical could happen to move the project forward.

So once again, Josh found himself traveling to a client meeting, getting himself ready to fight for his company's interests in a tough discussion. But his heart was not in it. He was confident that he knew what the client was going to say, and he certainly knew what his side was going to say—they had said it often enough, so it was getting pretty dull.

Typically, he would have a last-minute briefing call from his boss to make sure he knew exactly what to say and how to respond to the client's tactics. Sure enough, just before he walked into the client's office, his phone rang.

WHAT'S THE OBJECTIVE?

"Josh, you are on speakerphone," said his boss. "I have our CEO here with me in the office." If the CEO had walked into his boss's office things were definitely getting serious.

Josh's boss asked him the question he had asked just before every one of these meetings: "What is your objective for this meeting?" so Josh knew what to expect. Even though he knew the CEO was on the call he knew that he was on solid ground when he said, "We need to make sure they know that the development costs for the next stage will be billed to them and that we will retain all intellectual property rights for new developments. We need to stay firm on the 50/50 cost sharing for the testing of the new power system, and push for full contract signature by the end of this fiscal year."

> *"Your objective for this meeting is to get this project unstuck and back on track."*

There was a silence at the other end of the phone for a while with some muffled discussion in the background. Then the CEO came on the line. "Josh, this project is all about us becoming a key player in the most advanced high-speed rail system in the world between two cities of global importance. If you ask me, your objective for this meeting is to get this project unstuck and back on track because right now it doesn't seem to be going anywhere fast. Does that make sense?"

"That makes absolute sense to me," said Josh, wisely deciding to agree with his CEO.

The meetings with the client normally started with a short discussion of the agenda to ensure it was correct and that everyone's expectations were set. As they went around the table Josh, surprisingly, became more and more relaxed. His CEO had just given him a corporate credit card to do whatever he wanted to get the project back on track. Far from increasing the pressure, it had relieved it. Josh remembered that his job, in fact everybody's job, worked out a lot better if it was fun, too.

ANYTHING TO ADD?

"Anything you want to add to the agenda today, Josh?" asked the leader of the client team.

"There is something, actually," said Josh. "This isn't really a standard agenda item, but just before this meeting I had a call from our CEO. It has absolutely helped me focus." A few people smiled, and all were paying attention to what Josh was saying. "We should all be very excited to be responsible for creating the world's most advanced high-speed train system, but we have instead spent so much time and energy trying to manage problems. That does not seem to be working out too well. Maybe we should try to solve these problems rather than manage them.

> **"I just can't see us getting this thing moving the way it should."**

"To be frank, for me this project is not a lot of fun right now—but it should be great fun for us all. If we can't find a way to bring some fun and perspective into this project, I just can't see us getting this thing moving the way it should."

The project leader from the client side asked, "And that would work—how?"

"I don't have any magic wand, but I think we need to get out of these meeting rooms and get back in touch with what the project is all about," replied Josh. "How about we set our next meeting at our test track? We can look at the trial model and, you know, have some fun messing around with the simulator."

The client leader nodded slowly. "And then we could find out if we are actually on the same page in terms of how we see this thing working in reality?"

"Yes, we can," responded Josh. "Then if there are differences, we can focus in creating a single vision rather than spending all this time on details that don't matter if we can't get this thing moving soon."

FRESH AIR AND FOCUS

"I have no issue in trying to get some fresh air—and fresh thinking—on this problem," said the client. "A little bit of fun can only help."

A few weeks later both teams met at Josh's firm's testing site. His CEO was delighted at Josh's initiative and cleared his schedule to spend the full day with them. His big-picture perspective and obvious enthusiasm were infectious, bringing new energy to both teams.

The negotiations resumed, but the new perspective and the sense of fun and teamwork Josh's approach had brought to them made a huge difference in their progress.

SANDLER TAKEAWAYS FOR BOOTSTRAPPERS

1. **Fun is part of the mix.** Josh decided to bring fun into his sales project, and in so doing he tapped into the human side of his colleagues. He focused on the potential of the people to create something exciting and worthwhile rather than the problems they faced.

2. **Lead a sale; don't manage it.** Selling should mean taking responsibility for leading people toward a goal. Josh took on the responsibility to lead the teams of both companies out of the head-to-head skirmishing, breaking a dysfunctional pattern by using the fun side of his job to build human relationships with the people involved.

3. **Perspective is the salesperson's responsibility.** During a complex sale, there can be a lot of competing agendas. It can be easy to lose sight of the real objective. As the owner of the sale, it's your job to navigate the path toward a conclusion. Won't this get you closer to a satisfied prospect and a profitable deal?

4. **Speed is the measure of time taken toward a deal, not the time taken to cross items off a to-do list.** Salespeople need to apply their critical intelligence to make sure that they are not just "busy fools." They need to contribute and move things forward, not merely go through the motions.

CHAPTER 12

Lost in Transit

Or: An at-leaster finds out the real cost of making assumptions

S elling is a joint activity between you and the customer. When it works well, it feels like being a project manager responsible for driving a complex and difficult process where the goal is to make it easier for your customer to make the right decision.

It is easy, however, to focus on the process and forget the objective—in particular, to forget that even though it feels like teaming with your clients, the responsibility for driving the project is only ever with you, the seller.

Selling is a joint activity between you and the customer.

Getting lost in the tactical weeds of working with a client can be dangerous, as Mike found during a particularly grueling sales project.

Working for a jet engine manufacturer was a dream come true for Mike, who was selling Web-based IT into the civil aviation market. Putting thousands of aircraft full of people into the air every day around the world is so complicated and potentially risky that it's hard to imagine anyone setting out to run an industry like it, given the choice.

IT'S COMPLICATED

Often the companies who own the planes you sit in don't operate them. Sometimes they carry out some of their own maintenance, and sometimes they have other companies do it. Sometimes they hold a stock of spare parts, and sometimes the spares are held by the original manufacturer. Sometimes, if they are in a rush, they borrow parts from their direct competitors. On top of this, every single critical part on an aircraft has a set lifetime in operation. Whenever the aircraft gets used, somebody, somewhere, has to take note of that use and keep count as to when that part needs to be replaced. Like I said—it's complicated.

> *There was no one person who could say "yes,"*
> *but there were dozens who could say "no."*

The software system Mike's firm sold was a good attempt to make the process a little less complicated. However, in order to make the project acceptable to a risk-intolerant industry, the company needed to get their first real customer on board and operational. As with most new ideas, there was a "rush to be second"—and no rush at all to be first—with a system that needed the airline and aircraft maintenance companies to rewrite their operations manuals.

Mike's firm found a great prospect—one who understood the benefits the firm could help generate and who knew that the pains of adoption would be worth it. The issue in this type of sale was that, since it affected so many departments, anyone in the airline's leadership team could stop it. Since the business case was complex, they also needed their teams on the ground to sign off. There was no one person who could say "yes," but there were dozens who could say "no."

KEEP DEMONSTRATING UNTIL THEY SURRENDER

This meant lots of demonstrations of Mike's system, each one slightly tailored to the particular technical audience. Mike's champions inside the airline played their part by organizing meeting after meeting with every department in the organization and making sure that the right people attended.

After having done many of these demonstrations, Mike was quite blasé about handling tough questions and proving the value of the system, both to the whole business and to the people on the ground responsible for keeping the fleet flying. So when he was asked to fly down to their head office to "show some of the operations people what this is all about," it seemed like it would be easy.

As requested, Mike turned up right on time, just before 4:00 p.m. one Friday afternoon, and was pleased to see his number one supporter waiting for him at reception. Mike and his champion chatted away for a few minutes. Then he opened the door to the meeting room, and Mike's heart almost stopped beating. Instead of a team of operations planners and engineers expecting to see a system demo, Mike was confronted by all 12 members of the airline's operations committee—basically the leadership of the entire airline. The table in front of them was strewn with half-eaten sandwiches and dirty coffee cups— evidence of a long day of internal discussion. Twelve pairs of tired and irritated eyes focused on Mike. It was clear that he was the only thing standing between them and the weekend.

PREPARED, BUT FOR THE WRONG MEETING

It was not a welcoming audience. They had no idea why Mike was there. They had been given nothing to describe the project except a one-line item on the agenda, no background and nothing describing the objectives they were all trying to achieve. From the minute he strolled into the room, Mike was holding 12 people hostage. Nothing he could have said would have made them engage with the project.

"So, Mike, can you talk the guys through the business case for this project?" said his champion, taking his seat. If he had had an hour's notice Mike could have done it standing on his head. He and his team had a stack of charts, illustrations and scenarios all prepared that showed a great business case, but right at that moment none were accessible to him. What was more critical was that he was on autopilot. This was supposed to be a technical demo to bring operations people on board, and shifting gears from that to presenting a big-picture business rationale to the client's senior team was a step too far. Mike had probably done worse presentations, and perhaps his hostages had seen worse too, but it is safe to say that nobody left that room convinced.

> *From the minute he strolled into the room,*
> *Mike was holding 12 people hostage.*

It was Mike's fault. His champion had done nothing wrong—except possibly not giving Mike a better briefing about the meeting. He had grown used to working with Mike and his company and had forgotten to tell them that this particular meeting was important. Mike had always put on a great show in the past, so he had relaxed slightly too much with his champion and had slipped into treating him like an extension of his own team.

"I'M THE FUEL GUY"

Despite this shambles, the project rumbled on until it eventually wound its way up to the Really Important Person who held the purse strings. If this person liked it, the project was approved; if not, it was dead in the water.

By now Mike had done about a dozen demos of his superb IT system to this organization. Having survived the horror of being thrown into a meeting of the executive team without preparation, you had better believe that he was super-organized for this meeting. He was not intending to crash and burn again.

The meeting started 30 minutes late, but eventually Mike was ushered into the presence of the Really Important Person.

"Ah," this person said, "you are the guy on the fuel project."

Mike was not sure how to tell Really Important Person that he was wrong.

Mike may have actually said, "Ah-ha!" out loud.

"No, I am the IT guy," he said. "I am on the IT project. We want you to buy our IT system."

The Really Important Person looked at him briefly, then, deciding that there was no point in talking to him directly. He spoke over his shoulder to Mike's internal champion: "I thought this was the fuel guy."

"This is the fuel guy," said Mike's champion.

"I'm the IT guy," Mike repeated, but with less conviction than before. If both these guys thought he was a fuel guy, perhaps he was the one who was wrong.

The three of them looked at each other for a while, and then Mike's champion said to the Really Important Person, "If we buy his IT thing, we will be able to cut our fuel use by about one percent."

Mike may have actually said, "Ah-ha!" out loud. Despite the fact that his super system did about 25,000 astonishing things, as far as the client was concerned Mike's firm had one value—it would allow them to reduce their fuel costs.

"Oh, right. I am the fuel guy," Mike said, nodding.

SANDLER TAKEAWAYS FOR BOOTSTRAPPERS

1. **What is the purpose of this meeting?** Next time you go to a meeting without checking that you actually know what outcome the customer expects, give yourself a reality check. It is not the customer's job to make sure that you are not wasting your time.

2. **Stop guessing; start asking.** If you don't understand the reasons that someone wants to buy from you, you are guessing. Don't only check with your own team; far too often salespeople believe they have a great strategy internally, but that can really be nothing more than "group guessing."

3. **The prospect's reason for buying beats your reason for selling.** You may think you know why the prospect wants to buy your thing—after all, you have to believe that you have a great solution to his problems—but it is never a waste of time digging into his reasons to buy.

4. **Prepare, prepare, prepare.** Good preparation is probably the best investment you can make in sales. Often, this preparation

requires nothing more than a clear Up-Front Contract: what does the prospect expect from this meeting, what do you need and what will be the probable next steps if this meeting works out? Professional salespeople don't guess—they verify.

5. **Keep out of the weeds.** Even when you are deep into the technical or process details of how a product will work for the client, it is your mission to constantly keep his eyes on the prize: solving his pain in a way that makes commercial sense for both of you.

CHAPTER 13

Activity or Progression?

Or: An at-leaster finds out the difference between busy meetings and productive decisions

S ome businesses are fast, dynamic and constantly changing. They are exciting to work in and offer new challenges on a daily basis. Some are less so. Andrea felt that she worked in the "less so" category. When people asked her what she did, she never felt proud to say, "I sell paper products." A lot of her time was spent in meetings. Sometimes they were productive, often they were not. It took a major review with a major client to learn that the responsibility for making the difference lies with her.

Andrea was responsible for her firm's sales into the food industry. Even though the business was large and produced significant profit, there was always the feeling that they were at the bottom of the food chain when it came to driving new ideas into the market. The owners of the food brands spent millions on marketing, new product launches, flavor research and a dozen other things before the mundane world of paper packaging made it to their radar screen.

> *There was always the feeling that they were at the bottom of the food chain when it came to driving new ideas.*

This time, Andrea, VP of sales for food and beverage for her firm, felt there was a chance to make an impact with their biggest client, a fast-growing baked goods producer that sold through high-end supermarkets and independent retailers.

THE ROCK-AND-ROLL WORLD OF MUFFIN WRAPPERS

The client was particularly well-known for its range of muffins, and the sales team was always looking for a competitive edge. Research said that one thing annoyed consumers more than anything else: they hated the crumby mess from pulling the wrapper off the muffins and they had pretty negative feelings about the often soggy piece of paper that remained. As Andrea was the first to admit, this was possibly not the most rock-and-roll industry in the world.

Another issue was the client's personnel. They liked to build consensus for making decisions, and they loved meetings. There were cookies and coffee at every meeting, and Andrea was sure that many of the people who attended would not have been there without the free baked goods. With this client, things never seemed to get done.

In a few days' time, Andrea and her team would be flying to meet the client's team to push a new process that would solve some of their problems and maybe even give Andrea's company a competitive story to tell in the market.

Heading out of town meant that Andrea needed to call in a favor from her mother to pick up the kids from school while she was gone. Her mother loved spending time with her grandkids, but always seemed to take these opportunities to take a swipe at Andrea's job.

WHAT'S THE PURPOSE OF THIS MEETING?

"Why do you go to all these meetings?" Andrea's mother asked her.

"We need to have a lot of meetings to get things done," Andrea said. "There are lots of decisions to be made in a deal like this."

"What is this big meeting all about? What is the 'big picture?'"

Andrea took a deep breath. "You know that when you pull the paper wrapper off a muffin and some bits of the muffin stay stuck to the wrapper?"

> *"What is this big meeting all about?"*

"Yes."

"The guys in the lab believe they have a new way of treating the paper so that it will hold its shape better during baking but peel away easier. You know, fewer crumbs."

"For muffin crumbs, you're flying for five hours?"

"Yup, for crumbs I am taking a five-hour flight. Fewer muffin crumbs means fewer customers with crumbs on their laps, and that means more people might buy more muffins, more often."

"What are you going to decide at this big meeting of yours?" asked her mother.

"Well," said Andrea, "this is not one of those meetings where we will make an actual decision. It's more about showing them where we are in terms of our development."

"So you won't decide anything?"

"YOU JUST DON'T UNDERSTAND"

"Mom, you just don't understand business." And that was the end of the conversation.

Although she was sometimes frustrated by her mother's simple view of the business world, Andrea could not shrug off her final question. What was the point of this meeting? If the meeting went well, what did she expect as a result? She had enough experience to know that the progression toward a final deal required more than good presentations and samples. Nothing would happen until the client made some decisions. While they were not in a place where they could expect a final decision, if the client was serious about the new packaging ideally he should be ready to make some moves.

The day before the trip, Andrea called her team together for a planning meeting.

"Everything about this product makes great sense for the client," she told them. "It might be more expensive than what the client is using right now, but if he is serious about tackling the problem, this is the best technical solution on the table. My biggest concern is that we have gotten ourselves into a pattern of pitching things to the client and hoping that he might do something. I am getting a little frustrated at this 'pitch and pray' strategy."

The three team members nodded in agreement, but did not

"I am getting a little frustrated at this 'pitch and pray' strategy."

offer any great insights as to how they could change the pattern. The silence was not inspiring.

"OK," continued Andrea, "what do we think the client team wants from the meeting tomorrow?"

IT'S OBVIOUS!

"They told us what they want," said Don, the technical development manager. "They want to find out how we are doing on the development side."

"Great. Specifically, what do we think they want to know?"

"Mainly, they probably care most about adhesion and resistance to contamination, I guess," said Don.

"Sounds reasonable that they should be focused on those, I suppose. Anything else?"

Martina, their materials technician, tended not to speak up at meetings like this, but this time she seemed compelled to contribute. "All the questions we've been getting from them lately are about forming and rigidity. I think their hot buttons are around getting a case that can be pressed into shape easily and not collapse like wet tissue when consumers peel it off."

"Good stuff," smiled Andrea. "Anything else?"

The technical team shrugged and shook their heads.

"So, we think their big concerns are rigidity, contamination, shaping and adhesion?" Three heads nodded in response.

It was a start, but not the whole story. The last thing Andrea wanted to do was to turn up at the meeting, have her and her team talk for hours, eat too many free cookies and then fly home.

WHAT DO WE WANT?

"All right then, what do we want to get from this meeting?" Andrea asked.

"We want to make sure they understand our progress," said Don.

"That is certainly a good thing, but if this meeting were to go really well, what would we love to see happen?"

Martina was the first to respond. "We would love for them to tell us if they think our forming and rigidity are better than anything else they have seen in the market, or if we are just kidding ourselves."

> ### "What do we want to get from this meeting?"

Don nodded, then added, "We always get it in the neck when they leave all the decisions until the last minute and put the pressure on us to make up for the time they lost in the first place."

Everyone in the team recognized that situation.

"All good stuff," said Andrea. "Is there a decision we want them to make at this meeting, or is it show and tell?"

"There is one big decision they need to make," said Don. "They need to let us know if this change would be made for the launch of the winter product range. For us to hit their timelines, we need an answer by the end of the month."

This meeting coming up had all the hallmarks of being difficult. The client probably expected them to appear, show a bunch of presentation slides, tell them everything they knew about ways to solve the problem and then shuffle off home and wait to be called. Andrea did not relish the idea of spending all that time and effort on another "pitch and hope" meeting. Besides, she had her mother to impress.

GET THE AGENDAS ON THE TABLE

Rather than send the normal agenda email over to the client, Andrea picked up the phone and spoke to the project leader on the client side. She explained that she was bringing her "A" team and that they would be able to make solid decisions on their side right during the meeting. She explained that her firm would need some decisions to be made by the client in order to make the established deadlines, and she asked if the client could invite everyone on their side who had a stake in the project.

At the meeting, Andrea stood up, smiled at the attendees and said, "Before we begin, I want to thank you for inviting us here today. We appreciate it." She looked down at her notebook and read out the list of things she and her team had drawn up before they left their office. "From your side, I think you want to understand if we can meet your expectations on resistance to contamination, package rigidity to stop the baking wrapper collapsing after use, ease of shaping for the production line and, of course, anti-adhesion to tackle the whole muffin-crumb issue. Do you mind if I ask if we have that right, or if there is anything we have missed?"

There was a little bit of discussion, but on the whole the client team was happy that all their points were on the table.

> **"Do you mind if I ask if we have that right, or if there is anything we have missed?"**

"From our side," Andrea continued, "we hope to talk about possible timelines and deadlines for decisions. Can I ask if we can discuss what your expectations are in terms of a possible market launch?"

There was no rush to respond to this point, so Andrea let a little silence do the talking. Eventually the marketing leader from the client team spoke up. "If this thing goes ahead, I can tell you when we need to start getting the message out there to the market. Would that work?"

"That would be a huge help to us, thank you," Andrea said. "We would also love your feedback on what you have seen from us so far. Are we showing you anything that makes sense?" She took the group of nodding heads as a *yes* from the client. She pushed on.

IT'S A DECISION THING

"I don't want to get ahead of ourselves here," Andrea continued, "but, if this meeting works out, we can either decide to move ahead to a production trial or we can agree to push this thing onto the back burner for now. Would that make sense from your side?"

The senior project leader from the client side seemed happy with those as possible outcomes. "We are ready to make some decisions on this idea. If we move forward, trials would be the next obvious step. But let's have a look at what you have for us today before we do anything else."

From here, Andrea took a back seat as her technical team presented their results and dealt with questions. The decision on whether to proceed to a production trial happened by itself, and the meeting began to close. As people glanced at watches and tidied up their papers, Andrea got to her feet again.

"Everyone, this has been a great meeting from our side. I appreciate your openness and input. Before we head out, I would like to confirm that between now and the next time we meet, we will get you a date for delivery of our production trial materials and a pricing estimate. I think, from your side, the big thing is a date for the actual trial and then some idea of when consumer tests will take place. Have I got that right?"

There was a chorus of people grunting their agreement.

"Great. If the trial works and the pricing makes sense, then we may well have a winner here."

The leader of the client team walked them to the front door.

"You know," he said, "we like dealing with your firm. You're an organized bunch."

Andrea smiled; the only thing better than hearing that was the satisfaction she would feel when she told her mother that the meeting had actually decided something.

SANDLER TAKEAWAYS FOR BOOTSTRAPPERS

1. **Use an up-front contract.** Few tools will change your sales life more than the up-front contract. If you get the prospect's expectations, your expectations, target outcomes, decisions and times onto the table, you will find that not only will the meetings be far more productive, you will also earn the reputation of being someone with whom people like doing business.

2. **Have meetings to make decisions.** Nothing kills a sale more than a prospect who never decides. Every meeting you have should end with a decision, and every major decision should be identified and placed on the agenda far in advance of the discussion. If prospects are not told that you are meeting with them in order to make a decision together, then you have no right to be surprised when they decline to do so.

3. **Salespeople have rights, too.** Your job is never to pitch and beg. You invest heavily in trying to solve the pains of your clients. The time, energy and knowledge you put into a deal deserves reciprocation on the side of the prospect. When you give prospects something from your side, even if it's nothing more than your time, you should ask yourself, "What will they contribute?"

4. **Train your prospects to misbehave.** If you teach your clients and prospects that it is good buyer behavior to treat your knowledge, energy and time as free gifts, then they will act as though that is the case. If you consistently act like a professional business partner, trading value at every meeting, then you can often train them to respond to you in that way.

CHAPTER 14

Pretty Smart, Really Stupid

Or: An at-leaster has the choice between trying to look smart and actually being smart

Technical knowledge can be a fantastic tool for a salesperson, but it can also be a sales killer if it is not deployed with caution. Simon knew a lot about his industry, but his inability to manage that knowledge caused him—and everyone around him—a lot of problems.

Simon was in love with his product and his industry. This was no mean feat, as he worked in an industry that most people found dull: industrial fastening systems. His firm made fixing systems that kept other components in place, often in extreme conditions and for important components. If you needed a fuel pipe to connect to the engine of a jet fighter flying at twice the speed of sound, or if you needed to secure a valuable computer sensor to a deep-sea robot submarine, then you called Simon's company.

> *His grasp of the technical side of his product made him the favorite of his engineering support team.*

Simon was not a trained engineer, but his grasp of the technical side of his product made him the favorite of his engineering support team. He read everything in the trade press. When he went to trade shows, he would make the time to attend technical seminars about new advances in technology. In any conversation with his peers or the commercial people with his clients, he could explain a lot of the technical parts of the problems his products could overcome. This made him a valuable part of his team and a great support to his clients. More than once clients had referred to Simon's surprising depth of knowledge, and their positive feedback was a real confidence booster to him.

AT THE CUTTING EDGE

One of his newer clients was struggling with a tough challenge, which Simon knew was at the cutting edge of the technical capability for the industry. When he had a meeting with the project manager from the client side, Simon brought value to the discussion because he had participated in an online webinar on this subject just a few weeks prior. He mentioned to the project manager possible ways of resolving some of the challenges. The conversations went well, and Simon was invited along to one of the client's project team meetings to share his thoughts.

Simon felt great at being invited into the heart of his client's team for the project meeting. He was introduced by his main contact, and quite quickly the meeting began to focus on the technical challenges they faced in Simon's area. The team discussed the lack of progress on the issue. Then Simon was invited to contribute.

Simon quickly recapped the problem as he understood it, made sure he had an accurate understanding, and then outlined the latest thinking on how this could be addressed. He had understood the content of the webinar pretty well, and since he had taken part in so many technical seminars and trade show presentations he had a lot of additional knowledge he could share. The audience was impressed and gave him their undivided attention. For almost all of them this was the first time they had met Simon, and he was creating a good first impression.

Some of the project team started asking questions about the type of solution Simon was suggesting. At first Simon was on pretty solid ground and coped well, but soon the questions became more specific, getting to the limits of what Simon had learned in his reading. By this time only Simon and the engineers in the room could follow the conversation. It slowly occurred to Simon that the people in the room did not see him as a helpful salesperson with some intelligent ideas; they were looking at him as though he were an engineer fully qualified in the field.

DECISION TIME

As the level of the discussion increased, Simon was faced with a tough decision. Should he stop the technical side of the discussion, tell the group that he needed to bring in his engineering team, and admit that he was out of his depth? That would certainly have been the smart thing to do, but it would have meant losing face in front of an important group at a major customer.

Simon chose not to do the smart thing. Instead, he kept talking. His answers and comments became more wooly and evasive. The room could see from the faces and comments of their own engineers that they were getting skeptical about Simon's real level of knowledge. Eventually, after one question, their senior engineer just looked away from Simon, nodded and picked up his phone to check emails. The conversation was over, and with some embarrassment Simon's contact thanked Simon for coming to the meeting and making such a valuable contribution.

> *Simon chose not to do the smart thing. Instead, he kept talking.*

He was not asked back.

ONCE IS DUMB, TWICE IS PLAIN STUPID

Simon knew what he did know, and he also knew what he did not know. What happened to Simon that day was that he took a good relationship and some valuable insights into a customer's problem and blew both of those advantages away with some pretty dumb behavior.

You could say that this was a simple error made through inexperience, naivety, and a desire to look good in front of important decision makers, and you would possibly be right in excusing Simon for his mistake. However, the real tragedy happened six months later.

Simon found himself working with a small client who lacked a lot of the expertise his big budget customers had. Since Simon appeared to have a huge amount of practical experience, they became more and more dependent on him for advice and guidance. Again, he found himself in a situation where his desire to help the client and his need to have the client see him as an expert outstripped his actual knowledge. This time the client lacked the experience to filter Simon's input, and they made some critical decisions based on Simon's suggestions, some of which turned out to be bad calls. The issues caused by this escalated to Simon's bosses and led to the two companies not working together anymore. Simon did not lose his job—he did not even lose any responsibility. But from then on, for the many years that Simon worked for that firm, whenever promotion was discussed Simon's name was never considered. During one internal meeting about promotion, Simon's boss was asked his opinion about Simon's professional potential. "Well," said his boss, "sometimes Simon can be living proof that it is possible to be well-educated and bright but sometimes quite stupid under pressure."

SANDLER TAKEAWAYS FOR BOOTSTRAPPERS

1. **Intelligence is not what you know, but the judgment you apply in making decisions.** One of the real challenges many people face is recognizing when it is time to make a decision. In Simon's case, it never occurred to him that he should make a decision about what to do when he knew his discussions were getting into technically dangerous areas—areas where he was out of his depth. He kept talking without thinking.

2. **Don't forget what your real job is.** Because Simon knew he would get praise and positive feedback for sharing his technical know-how, he kept repeating the same behavior. It felt good to be the smartest guy in the room. Simon did not think through what his real purpose was when working with clients. As a salesperson, his true job was to find problems, not rush into offering solutions.

3. **Are you looking for praise or for a good deal?** Very often in sales you have the tough decision whether you want to leave the room with the prospect's good opinion or with a deal.

Sales is no place to find approval. That is why you should have a personal support network of friends and family. Your role in sales sometimes means that you have to deliver short-term disappointment to prospects in order to reach a successful conclusion.

4. **Free consulting is worth every penny it costs.** Your job is to use the product knowledge you have to progress a sale. If it enhances your credibility in the eyes of the prospect, so much the better. But it can be a real danger if you allow sharing your expertise to become a means to feed your ego.

CHAPTER 15

Smart Focus

Or: Bootstrapping is about understanding the real problem, not what the prospect wants to discuss

I t might sound obvious that intelligence is a bootstrapping fundamental, but the sad fact is that huge amounts of sales time, energy and emotion are expended without much being dedicated to cold, practical thinking.

As the world of sales has become more and more process driven and the complexity of what we sell has increased, the profession of selling runs the risk of being "too busy to think." It is easy to fill your time and your mind with tasks and tactics, as these things are easy to focus on and normally are well within your comfort zone. This is particularly true when you have a dominant customer intent on driving the process. If you allow yourself to become the servant of the customer, then you are failing to act like a bootstrapper and may find yourself acting more like a robot.

Bootstrapping sales is not about filling in checkboxes, nor is it about running around keeping up with customer demands. It's about finding the way to create value for the client and profit for yourself.

Melissa had been regional sales manager for a mid-size building services firm for almost three years. Her firm managed the outsourced services for major building complexes like hospitals, schools and medical supply companies. It was a complex, competitive market, and over the years it had become strictly controlled in terms of performance targets and key performance indicators (KPIs). Contracts were complex and negotiations could be agonizingly detailed.

WHERE IS THE GOAL?

Thanks to a lot of hard work in her years as regional manager, Melissa got the recognition she deserved when she was called to a meeting at head office and told that they wanted her to take over the sales responsibility for the whole country. It was a huge step up, but it had the risk of being a poison chalice. Melissa's regional team had been performing well, but hers was the exception. When she started looking at the scope of her new area of responsibility, all she could find was problems. She walked into an avalanche of issues, everything from longstanding staff disciplinary grievances to customer complaints to problems with other departments that felt that sales had not been responding well to the rest of the organization.

Despite all of the organizational issues, Melissa still had to focus on driving sales. In order to help her prioritize her workload, she asked her new team for a list of the biggest opportunities they were pursuing with the actions required to close the deal. It soon became obvious that she had opened a Pandora's box, as scores of stalled opportunities flooded into her inbox. She had always managed her pipeline of potential business quite tightly, so she was amazed at the wave of emails that came from the national sales team. Many contained details of deals she had heard about from her colleagues, and a few were deals that she had heard referred to as already closed.

> *It's about finding the way to create value for the client and profit for yourself.*

She set aside an afternoon and called the salespeople responsible for the four or five biggest stalled deals. In every case, she heard different versions of the same story. Every opportunity was real enough—her firm was chasing a real deal—but the deals had become derailed over various issues in the late stages of approval by the client.

FASTEST ROUTE TO MONEY

Melissa was convinced that the fastest way to create success was to dive into the pile of blocked deals and turn some into done deals. Doing so would let her get closer to the new business areas she had taken over in her new role, it would generate credibility and trust from the team when they saw how committed she was to front line sales activity and, of course, it was expected to create some much needed revenue. Since she didn't know which of these potential deals could be quickly turned around, she started work on the top five simultaneously, getting the salespeople responsible to create a background brief and set up meetings with the key decision makers in each case.

> *She pushed decisions to other people and,
> rather than listening to problems, she quickly
> learned to insist that anyone bringing a problem
> had to bring options for resolving it.*

Almost as soon as this was moving, her boss told her that two of the existing sales teams had to be merged into one with a 25 percent reduction in headcount. This was a major project in itself and, given the timescale involved, enough to take up all of Melissa's time. But there was no way she could stop her project on the stalled deals. All she could do was take a deep breath and keep moving.

The workload was punishing. To keep things moving, she focused on the bigger issues and let the details be handled by others. She pushed decisions to other people and, rather than listening to problems, she quickly learned to insist that anyone bringing a problem had to bring options for resolving it. Still the work and pressure increased. This showed when she had to have a meeting with the first and biggest of her stalled deals.

The salesperson responsible for this deal was happy to have her support and seemed to have kept every piece of documentation ever created on it—all of which he passed on to Melissa.

DETAIL, DETAIL, DETAIL

There were several previous contract drafts, scores of lengthy emails and a number of PowerPoint presentations, all of which impacted the reasons for the contract negotiations being stuck. Melissa was briefed that the client had a great eye for detail and expected the people he dealt with to be well-prepared.

Melissa certainly intended to prepare for the meeting. She

cleared a whole afternoon in her schedule to read all the background materials. But unfortunately a crisis caused by the merger of her sales teams blew up, and the afternoon was spent working with her HR team. She had some time the evening before the meeting, but since it looked as though the firm was about to miss forecast for the third quarter in a row, she ended up having a lengthy conference call with her CEO and CFO. She woke up early the next morning and read the initial proposal and the most recent emails, but this gave her only enough of an insight to realize how many complex issues had arisen during the contract negotiation.

The salesperson responsible for the account met her at her hotel to drive them to the meeting. "I spent all day yesterday on the phone to head office preparing for this meeting," he said. "I have about twenty questions for which I need answers."

Melissa nodded, replying, "I really only have one."

The meeting started well enough, although Melissa noted that the client had a huge pile of documents and files that obviously related to the proposal, with colored tabs and highlighter notes all over them. There was no way that Melissa would be able to hold her own in a detailed discussion with the client, and any attempt to do so would result in a fiasco.

Once the introductions were over and everyone sat down, she watched the client pick up the first document from the pile he had brought with him.

DOES THIS MAKE SENSE?

Before he had a chance to start, Melissa spoke. "I hope you don't mind me saying something before we begin."

The client peered at her over the top of his spectacles but said nothing.

"I have been looking at that huge pile of paper you have there, and I know that we have a pile every bit as big back in our office," she said. "But I thought it might make sense to give ourselves a bit of focus for today's meeting. From our side, all we are trying to do is to work out if your organization has a problem that we are well-positioned to resolve. If you do, and we can make it work in a way that makes commercial sense to both of us, we should find the way to move forward. If not, then it probably makes sense to stop these conversations and we should all find something else to do with our time. I hope that doesn't sound too harsh. Does that sound unfair?"

> *"That is the first sensible thing anyone from your company has said in over a year."*

The client stared at Melissa for what seemed like a lifetime. Melissa felt she had taken her best shot, and that anything she might say could only weaken her position. She lived with the discomfort of the silence.

Finally he nodded, put down his papers, and said, "That is the first sensible thing anyone from your company has said in over a year. We do want to move ahead on this, and almost all of the issues that are holding this back are legal points. It may well be that we have allowed ourselves to get a little lost in the weeds here."

Melissa agreed. "I am not a lawyer, so would it make sense for us to have our legal team talk directly to your contracts department rather than through us?"

The client chuckled, saying that he was no lawyer either and that he was getting nowhere shuttling back and forth between his contract lawyers and meetings with Melissa's company. They agreed to bring the two legal teams together and spent the rest of the meeting ironing out other items that seemed to be critical.

The two legal teams resolved their issues quickly once they could negotiate directly, and the deal moved to a close. It was Melissa's first success in her new role, and the approach she had taken in that deal became something of a hallmark in her style.

It can be easy to confuse complexity with intelligence. Melissa knew that the people who had been working on that deal were not lacking either knowledge or motivation, so she had to apply her own intelligence to understand exactly what the real business problem was. In this case, the open question was whether the value of the deal to the client was big enough for the client to resolve the detailed objections.

SANDLER TAKEAWAYS FOR BOOTSTRAPPERS

1. **You are not the servant of the customer.** You are your clients' partner, not their errand boy. If clients know everything and have complete understanding of what needs to be done, they probably would not need to have your involvement. You are an expert in your field and, in the true sense of the word, your company's representative. That can mean applying a touch of "everyday courage" and taking charge of a situation, even with a dominant prospect.

2. **Make time to think.** Selling is a thinking job, so you need to make time to use your critical intelligence in every sales situation. In a job that is full of tasks and deadlines set by other people, it is too easy to be overwhelmed and act only based on other people's agendas.

3. **What do your stakeholders expect?** Stepping back from your own role for a second to look at how you are doing things from a key stakeholder's perspective can be an invaluable technique. What guidance would your boss, your colleagues, your CEO or your partners give you in terms of setting your priorities?

4. **"Does this make sense?"** Not all prospects are good prospects. At least once in every sales project, stop and ask yourself if the deal makes sense, both for you and the prospect. Sharing this question with a prospect can be incredibly valuable. It shows you have not lost focus on the original objectives. It also goes a long way to proving you are a valuable business partner, not a conventional pitch-and-beg salesperson.

CHAPTER 16

Asleep at the Wheel

Or: An at-leaster is confused about what "owning" an account really means

Bootstrap selling is all about accepting the responsibility to drive constructive change in how customers work and influencing their decisions to help them realize future benefits. It is not only putting in hours of work; it is investing the sales time, effort and emotional energy to find proactive ways to build the client's business.

Few things show the reality of sales more clearly than the idea that somebody "owns" a relationship. Ownership, accountability and commitment are vital in relationships with customers, but ownership defines behavior and a state of mind. It is not a job description.

Vicky had been working for her firm for more than 15 years. She had joined the company as a customer service executive straight from school. After more than five years behind a desk, she had moved into sales as an account manager when four of the salespeople quit her company suddenly to join a competitor.

> *Ownership defines behavior and a state of mind. It is not a job description.*

Vicky's company needed to plug the gaps in a hurry, and her good existing relationships with customers proved to be invaluable. She kept the links between her firm and their customers strong with frequent meetings, hand holding and a lot of tidying up after the sales guys left.

A REAL ASSET

Once the immediate crisis had passed, Vicky's company realized that she was a real asset as a wave of performance improvement projects swept their client base. Almost every one of their customers was suddenly knee deep in "re-engineering" their critical processes, and this meant a lot of work for key suppliers. Fortunately, Vicky had an unrivalled perspective on how the process of delivery worked, having spent years in customer service getting the nitty-gritty done.

All this brought her the lasting respect of her firm's leadership. Although she was never marked out for serious promotion, she was regarded as part of the company's DNA. Whenever her firm thought about making a major change to how they worked, Vicky was always in the mix. She was a "super user" when the new client relationship management system was installed. When the firm moved to a new automated ordering system, Vicky was asked to work with the launch customers to make sure that everything went well. The CEO made a point of talking to her whenever he visited.

Then she got a new boss.

NEW BOSS, NEW PERSPECTIVE

Her new boss, Paul, came from another industry entirely. For much of his career he had not even been in sales, but had been in operations and logistics. He took on the leadership of a business unit and found out that the sales side of the job was far and away the most fun and satisfying part of his role. When he had the chance to take on the regional sales leadership job, he leapt at it. Success there led to him being head-hunted by Vicky's firm as regional vice president of business development, and part of taking that job was becoming Vicky's boss.

Paul had been brought in because, in sales terms, the firm had stopped growing. Worse, as the market had become more mature, there was real pressure on margins. Profitability was being steadily eroded.

His first meeting with Vicky was quite reserved. Vicky had seen a few new leaders come and go, so she was not about to jump on a bandwagon just because it was new. Paul was open, curious and friendly. At the end of their first meeting, he summed up to Vicky, "You seem to have a real handle on what is going on inside the customer's organization, and from what I hear they hold you in high regard. What I would love to find out is how you see things developing over the next three years or so. Our friends in the marketing department think the speed with which the market

> *"Have we told them our perspective on where we want to go together?"*

is changing is only going to increase. Could you let me have some thoughts from your perspective on what we need to do differently in this market to stay ahead of the game?"

Vicky did not exactly gush with joy at the task, but took it on as yet another responsibility. She began to put together a short paper for Paul.

Paul called Vicky up a few weeks later, confused after he had read it. "Vicky, I have your paper here and I want to apologize. I made a mess of asking you for what I wanted."

Vicky was surprised and told Paul that she thought she had provided exactly what he had wanted.

MORE THAN THEIR SHOPPING LIST

"Well," said Paul, "this reads a little bit like a shopping list from your biggest customer. It's your thoughts I would value."

"But it's my job to look after the interests of my biggest customer," she said. "Surely his success is our success?"

Vicky's response surprised Paul, and not in a good way. Paul tried another tactic. "Vicky, it's great to see that our biggest customer has a clear vision for where he is going. We need to do the same thing. What is our plan with his company for the future? Have we told them our perspective on where we want to go together?"

Vicky's answer was long and vague—full of words but, to Paul's ear, without much content. They wound up the discussion with Paul feeling concerned about a lack of direction in their biggest account and Vicky thinking that Paul understood nothing about her market or the relationship with her biggest account.

Paul and Vicky had several conversations about growth. Most of these ended with Paul inviting Vicky to contribute her thoughts on growing the business and Vicky offering no real commitment to do anything specific.

WHY ROCK THE BOAT?

Vicky was busy anyway keeping up with her major client, so putting her mind or any effort into thinking about ways to grow sales was not much of a priority. In her heart, she did not believe that Paul had his priorities right. She knew that she was indispensable to the company due to her relationship with her major account. She felt that shaking things up would only lead to lots of hard work and risk without any clear benefit.

Eventually Paul took the initiative. He had Vicky set up a meeting with the CEO of her major account. Both Paul and Vicky went to the meeting, but within five minutes it was clear that Vicky was there as a courtesy. Paul and the CEO really hit it off. Vicky was stunned to hear Paul say, "We want to grow our business with you, but we don't know how to do that." She was doubly shocked when the CEO said, "To be honest, we never thought we were particularly important to you."

After that, Paul and the CEO of the client became the only two people actually meeting. Vicky sat on the bench watching.

Some good ideas came from that first meeting between Paul and the CEO, and some of those helped return the relationship to growth. Vicky went to some of the meetings, but not all, and within less than a year her role within the company had shrunk to being an administrator.

SANDLER TAKEAWAYS FOR BOOTSTRAPPERS

1. **You can work very hard in a sales role but still suffer from laziness.** Selling is about applying effort to your core role, and that is revenue generation. It may be that, like Vicky, your role is to focus on one or two major accounts, but if you see yourself as "owning" a relationship and forgetting why you have the responsibility in the first place, you cease to act like a bootstrapper and instead become a caretaker.

2. **You need to see the forest and the trees.** While somebody needs to keep an eye on the million and one things that happen with a complex customer or a challenging sales territory, that does not mean that you do not need to have the discipline to see the big picture of what is happening in the relationship and from where future business will come.

3. **What would you do if you were your boss?** There are few things more surprising than the perspective of somebody else looking at your area of business. It is amazing just how often you can find yourself saying, "I never thought of it like that." In the same way, it is an incredibly valuable practice to imagine yourself in someone else's shoes taking a good look at your sales situation.

4. **Why hide your ambitions from your customer?** Prospects and clients are human beings, too. If they know that you see them as an important part of your future, they might just be willing to help you get there. This does not mean that you share every part of your strategy with them, and it definitely does not mean you tell them that you are dependent on them. However, remember that they will plan based on their assumptions about your future business dealings. Unless you tell them what your projections for the future are, how will they know?

CHAPTER 17

The Importance of Being Flexible

Or: A bootstrapper finds a way through the sales fog

I f selling was a case of simply presenting a collection of the features and benefits, you could have a robot doing it by now. As one of the oldest sales adages in the world goes, "Telling isn't selling."

Selling requires you to guide your clients through the sometimes difficult experience of investigating what their real problems are, then finding the way to fix them—hopefully through working with you. It is increasingly rare for the sales process to be a simple case of moving from point A to point B in a straight, well-defined path. Very often, as salespeople work with their clients, they find themselves slightly lost, like wandering around in the fog. They're not sure where they are going until, through mutually productive dialogue, they find that it makes sense for both to head off in an entirely new direction—toward point C.

Scott found himself in this sales fog when he was called in by a large food manufacturing firm to help them sort out a production planning problem costing them millions in lost orders and forcing them to hold onto surplus stock that never seemed to move.

PEERING THROUGH THE SALES FOG

Scott's firm was highly specialized and provided integrated IT control systems for production, hardware for physically moving materials around automatically and consultancy services. When it came to solving problems around production planning, Scott's firm was a great team to have on your side.

At the first meetings with the client, Scott spent a lot of time learning how the current production system was working. Being a well-trained sales professional, he did everything he could to define the costs that the client had incurred thanks to things going wrong. The client was not shy about sharing this information with Scott.

> *It is increasingly rare for the sales process to be a simple case of moving from point A to point B in a straight, well-defined path.*

The situation was even more promising when Scott found out that his main contact had actually bought and implemented Scott's solution in his role with a previous company. He was selling to someone who had previously been a client of his firm, had seen his firm produce great results and, since he was quite new to his role, was also focused on delivering results as quickly as possible.

After a few exploratory meetings Scott had confirmed some great facts about the client's company. First, they had a problem costing them a high seven-digit figure. Second, the project had the blessing of the COO. Third, there was a budget allocated to resolve the problem. Although Scott could not get that exact number, he knew that the client fully understood how much his firm was likely to charge based on previous experience. It was a dream situation for a salesperson.

FOUR KILLER FACTS

The leadership of Scott's firm ran a process called the quarterly business review (QBR). Members of the sales team had to present their pipeline of opportunities and be able to discuss the key ones. Scott's presentation on this deal was a simple statement of his four killer facts: "They have a seven-figure problem, they have a budget to fix it, the key project champion has worked with us before and they are in a hurry."

It was a good presentation, and Scott's four killer facts brought his leadership team on board immediately. The only fly in the ointment came from Scott's head of finance, when he asked how Scott felt instinctively about the opportunity. Scott hadn't planned for this question. He had not even considered listening to his own gut feeling—the four killer facts were so clear and compelling that other considerations seemed not to matter.

The project got off to a great start. With the active collaboration of the client, a project plan was drawn up, a business case generated and initial demonstrations completed successfully. A draft proposal was created, and the project champion presented the concept to his board.

RADIO SILENCE

Then the project went very quiet. The feedback on the board meeting was not very detailed, but it was clear that the project champion had been told to do more work before it would be approved. Scott found that it was taking longer for the client to get back to him, and the project showed all the symptoms of one that was stalling badly.

Things did not stop completely, but the relationship got into a routine of long silences punctuated by short bursts of intense activity.

By his next quarterly business review Scott's fantastic opportunity had become a bit of a joke within the firm. Again, it was Scott's head of finance who seemed most interested. "Scott," he said, "this should be a great deal, a simple case of getting from point A to point B. I am really curious why it is not proceeding. I am supposed to spend some time every year meeting clients and prospects. Would it make sense for me to sit in on your next meeting?"

> *"Are you sure that we are a good fit to help you address the problems you are having?"*

By then, Scott was happy for any support, and the meeting was set up. When Scott, his finance leader and the client sat down together, Scott was surprised by the relaxed approach his finance guy took. He showed no real interest in reading up on the details of the project, and to Scott's eyes he seemed quite unprepared.

FINDING THE CHOKEPOINT

Almost immediately Scott's head of finance dived into the discussion. "You know, when Scott brought us this opportunity, we all thought that this would move pretty fast," he said. "From our understanding there was a clear problem, a good fit for our solutions and a live project to get things done. I know Scott and the team have put a lot into this from our side and that you have personally been in charge of rolling out our solution in another company, so I wonder what the issues might be. Are you sure that we are a good fit to help you address the problems you are having?"

At this, the client started to open up. It soon became obvious that there was considerable opposition to the project internally. Specifically, it turned out that although there were a lot of similarities between this project and the one the client had resolved before, there were also some considerable differences.

"Your system needs to have some pretty accurate demand forecast in order to make it run," said the client. "But our own sales teams keep saying that they cannot get a workable forecast from our customers. I know your system works, but there are some tough roadblocks."

Scott's finance leader nodded. "We had the same situation when we installed our new finance system," he said. "I was sure that the system I had seen before would work for us, but it took a long time to get the thing working. I remember our CEO saying to me, 'If you only have a hammer, every problem looks like a nail. Forget about the solution and go back to the problem.' I wonder if that is something we might consider?"

WHERE WE NEED TO GO

"Let's try this," said the client, standing up in front of the whiteboard in his office. "Let me show you how things work now and where we need to go."

The client quickly drew up a diagram showing how information was collected and used throughout his company's production planning and manufacturing system. The three of them then started working on the diagram to look at different ways things could be managed.

The short meeting that had been planned turned into a four-hour workshop. At the end of this session, Scott said, "Seems like we were trying to force a round peg into a square hole. We might be better off using some of the smart systems we have developed to produce a demand forecast based on historical data before we do anything else. What do you think?"

The client nodded. He had wanted a fast project that solved the whole problem straight away. But there was no denying it; without reasonable data going in at the front end, no system was going to be able to deal with the production issues.

"Tell me more about the forecasting systems you have," the client said.

THE REAL PROBLEM

The production planning project was put back on the shelf, and a new project was launched to focus on forecast accuracy. Scott's team worked with the client's sales leaders to get them on board, and within a few weeks it was approved in outline and led to a profitable and successful phase one, paving the way the following year for a successful implementation of the full system.

Having spent several miserable months lost in the sales fog trying to get from point A to point B, it took some fresh thinking to realize that the actual path back to progress was in a different direction.

SANDLER TAKEAWAYS FOR BOOTSTRAPPERS

1. **It's the problem, not the solution.** Putting all the effort into driving a particular solution can lead to forgetting the problem being addressed in the first place. One thing to remember constantly in sales is that you can either find customers for your solution or you can find solutions for your customers. The smart way is to find the solutions your customers need.

2. **The easiest person to convince can be yourself.** Big facts can disguise the real situation. Scott's four killer facts did more to blind both his team and the client to the real situation than they did to illuminate it. By repeating the same four facts, Scott had failed to use his instincts. Although all the facts were accurate, he had not used his instinctive judgment to assess what was happening. The human mind is the most complex system in the world for absorbing and analyzing facts, and failing to use that instinctive process was where Scott got dragged down the wrong path.

3. **Expect to walk through sales fog.** If customers' problems were so straightforward, they would not need salespeople to solve them. You should anticipate that most meaningful sales journeys will take you through a foggy patch where the problems need a little more focus and the fit of your solutions needs a little bit more verification.

4. **Be continually curious.** Whenever you find yourself in a situation where you cannot see the way forward, genuine, open curiosity tends to offer the fastest route to a productive solution—and the way to express that curiosity is with the client directly.

CHAPTER 18

Everyday Cowardice

Or: An at-leaster pays the price for picking
what seemed to be the easy way forward

Many people who care about success spend time and money learning new ways to improve their sales capabilities. But the best techniques and methodologies in the world are of no value if you fail to put them into practice. When you do try and apply new ideas, it should come as no surprise that there are some obstacles to overcome—and one of the strongest obstacles to doing what you know you should is the horrible but real concept of cowardice.

Some people define courage as the ability to do something even when afraid. Cowardice, then, is knowing something needs to be done but allowing fear to stop you from doing it. Typically cowardice is shown through a bad choice made under pressure in a moment of weakness. These tiny bursts of cowardice take up only a few moments of a person's working life, but can have a huge impact on a career.

> *The best techniques and methodologies in the world are of no value if you fail to put them into practice.*

Kate faced this sort of moment during the biggest sales opportunity she had ever had. She was very knowledgeable in her field of security systems—the type used in high-value buildings such as banks or airports, combining cameras, swipe cards, fingerprint recognition and other increasingly smart technologies. She was also a great presenter and found it easy to talk to people—a great combination of capabilities for a salesperson and one that had made her well regarded by her company. Her understanding of how her firm's systems could provide "intelligent security" was the main reason her bosses asked her to take on the sales relationship for their fastest-growing client.

TRUCKLOADS OF CASH

The client managed the difficult process of controlling the physical distribution of cash around the world. Planes and trucks full of cash were on the move constantly, and at any given time the exact value of every consignment needed to be accessible by many different people and every load had to be kept safe. The company was growing very quickly due to its ability to manage the global flow of cash more tightly and at a lower cost than any of the established players. This control and low cost was due to using the latest technology, which companies such as Kate's could provide.

Like the top professionals at a lot of cutting-edge companies, the decision makers at this client's company were demanding. If they asked a question, they expected it to be answered straight-away by the person who was sitting opposite them. The phrase, "Let me get back to you," did not win any prizes with them.

Kate's knowledge and enthusiasm had prompted her management to ask her to take on the sales responsibility for this client. Some people in her company, though, thought she was a little young and inexperienced for the responsibility. In fact, her company's leadership team was aware that they were running a risk by asking Kate to sit in the driver's seat with this client, but the risk seemed worth it so long as they gave her the support she needed.

Before every meeting with the client, Kate's boss would give her a call to make sure that she had everything she needed, that she had a good game plan for the meeting and that she knew that she had the support of her company. He was a good boss, and she looked forward to the regular call she had with him as soon as she finished any major meeting with this client.

> The phrase, "Let me get back to you,"
> did not win any prizes with them.

WORK THE PLAN

On this particular day, Kate had to meet with the client to discuss the next phase of a major project that would be of huge value to her firm. It was not only high value in financial terms, but it would also mean that her company had a partner in launching a new technology into the market. In her pre-meeting call with her boss, Kate had discussed how she expected the meeting to go and had worked out with him how to handle potentially difficult subjects, such as penalty payments that her company would be liable for if there were any failures in their systems and reduced pricing per site as the system was rolled out across the client's international network.

Kate managed the meeting well. She presented her firm's pricing proposal and backed up her ideas with solid logic. She defended her company's record on performance and made sure that any penalties her firm would be liable for would reflect actual costs the client had incurred. She was well-prepared, confident and professional.

Things went according to Kate's plan throughout the meeting, and even the issues that she had expected to be difficult seemed to be resolved without too much drama. She made concessions on some points, but nothing beyond the expectations of her firm. She was looking forward to making the post-meeting call to her boss.

Often, toward the end of a meeting, members of the client team would come up with an idea that would need input from someone else in their company. Meetings would end with them saying something like, "Let's ask so-and-so what he thinks about this." They would all troop around their offices looking for some new person's opinion on the project. Kate was fine with this as it seemed to create a new relationship for her firm every time it happened.

NEW FACE

This time the client said, "This will be a major project for us, and it will need our CFO to sign off on it. Maybe we should give him a heads-up now so that he can see what we are doing before it lands on his desk as a budget request." Everyone in the meeting agreed, particularly Kate, who was keen to get the support of the client's CFO early.

After a few phone calls, they tracked down the CFO who joined the meeting. Kate was happy to see her client's team summarize the project easily and quickly, showing her company in a great light. The CFO understood the whole idea almost immediately and asked Kate a few solid intelligent questions that showed he was thinking about how to make this project happen rather than challenging the idea.

The discussion was direct but positive, and the body language of the CFO indicated that he was happy with what he had heard. As the meeting broke up, the CFO said to the project team leader, "I can't see any big problems with this, it looks pretty solid. We probably want to make this a priority project as soon as the merger is complete."

Kate knew the client fairly intimately by this stage. This was the first time she had heard any suggestion that the client's company was about to go through a merger. In the long term, having a client involved in a merger is not automatically a bad thing as it can be a shortcut to having a much bigger client. On the other hand, Kate, like any other person with business experience, knew that when a firm goes through a merger, major decisions on any subject not directly related to the merger are put on hold as both companies dedicate their energy toward finding out more about their new partner and defining new ways of working.

THE MOMENT OF CHOICE

As she was walking out of the client building with her key contact, Kate could have turned and asked him about the comment the CFO had made about the merger. After all, it had been made in a meeting without any attempt to hide it, so it would have been easy to have raised the subject. But she didn't do it. She had had such a positive meeting and things were looking so great overall, that she didn't want to burst the bubble. She could always find out more sometime later. She chose not to do the tough thing.

A few minutes later she was on the phone to her boss. He was happy about the outcome of the meeting. He told her the head office team was proud of how she was managing such a demanding client and that she was doing great work. Kate knew that she should have told him about the mention of a merger, but again, she didn't want to be the bearer of bad news. She had become so used to the constant positive feedback from her company that throwing a wrench in the works was something she could not bring herself to do.

> *She chose not to do the tough thing.*

Everything moved forward on the project, and her firm saw this deal as being as good as done. Internally, the value of this contract was now being built into the financial forecasts.

News of the client's merger plans did not become fully public for another two months. Not surprisingly, when it was announced, Kate's firm was told that a final decision on the project would be put back until the merger was complete. Since this happened near the end of the financial year, it meant that Kate's division missed their performance target by a substantial margin.

In a last-ditch attempt to bring the deal in on time, Kate's own CEO called the CEO of the client. The client's CEO was sympathetic but could do nothing. "I'm really sorry if our merger is going to impact you, but you know how it is. We need to get this done before we move forward with your project. We assumed you knew all about the merger. It was never a secret."

Shortly after the reorganization that followed the merger, the deal with Kate's company took place. It was a great deal and Kate got a lot of credit for bringing it in, but she could not help but notice that increasingly her boss would attend client meetings with her and that she was no longer trusted to be the sole point of contact.

SANDLER TAKEAWAYS FOR BOOTSTRAPPERS

1. **Make the tough decision.** It is often tempting to take the easy way out when faced with a decision that needs you to tackle your own fears. In many sales situations, the only way forward is to tackle the short-term cowardice that may feel comfortable at the time but in reality brings long-term pain.

2. **Look for the problems.** When everything seems to be going well and there are nothing but blue skies ahead, it is still someone's responsibility to look out for problems. That responsibility lies with the salesperson.

3. **A plan is only as good as its execution.** Key account plans may be valuable tools for working out a sales strategy, but it is the actual behavior on the ground that makes the difference when it comes to sales effectiveness. The old phrase, "Planning is everything, the plan is nothing," is as true in sales as in any other sphere of activity. When a situation changes, your plan is out of date.

4. **Find the time to clear up a mess before it happens.** Often, salespeople rush a sale. They can skip critical steps and sometimes choose which facts to ignore. So many times sales problems arise because someone failed to act in time and in the right way. If there is one question you need to ask yourself on a daily basis, it is, "What has changed since the last time I spoke to the client?"

CHAPTER 19

Infectious Courage

Or: A bootstrapper relies on five
seconds of everyday courage to break
through with a hesitant prospect

F ear is contagious. Happily, the opposite is true, too. Behaving
in a fearless way is also infectious and confidence from a salesperson breeds confidence in a customer, as Alexander found
out when his project reached a critical stage. He knew that the
conventional path of "stand up and pitch features and benefits"
just would not wash.

There had been a lot of tension over this project. It involved
some new technology, some cutting-edge ideas and, on the whole,
a brand new way of tackling a business challenge that was costing
the industry a lot of money. Alexander had been working on this
project for months.

> *Confidence from a salesperson breeds confidence in a customer.*

Nobody had any doubt that the problem needed to be fixed. At the same time, few were convinced that the supplier's proposed solution was without risk. As is often the case with bold and creative ideas, there were a lot of questions about how things would work and how much risk there was for everyone. The customer was nervous about being a guinea pig and the first to make such a bold move. The supplier was nervous about moving forward with anything less than 100 percent commitment from the client.

DECISION TIME

Having had a series of meetings, several product demonstrations and some detailed project planning sessions, the customer was now ready to make a final decision. It was such a major decision that the customer's company brought their whole executive committee into the loop.

Meetings like this take a while to organize. It can take quite a bit of internal selling to ensure all the key players invest the time to do the relevant preparation. By the time the meeting came around, there was a lot of momentum behind the project and expectations were high.

Major projects tend to make people take a position. If you are asked to take part in reviewing a project proposal and then help make a decision, you are expected to provide an opinion. For very human reasons, some people pick a position emotionally then look for reasons to support it later. Some people on the client side in this case were in favor of the project. Some, however, were not. They had tough questions they wanted to put to Alexander and his team.

This meeting was so important that it had acquired a name of its own. It was called by everyone involved the "Go/No-Go" meeting.

PREPARE, PREPARE, PREPARE

Alexander and the team from his firm were thoroughly prepared. Prior to the Go/No-Go meeting, he had met with his strongest supporter within the customer's company to review his presentation. He wanted to make sure that there was nothing missing and that all of the major points were fully covered.

"You have hit about every point right on the nose," said his contact. "But even with all of this, you still need to be aware that there is some opposition internally to going down this route."

"What is the main thing people are concerned about?" asked Alexander.

"We are just not that driven by technology. To be honest, we have fallen flat on our faces more than once with big projects. We spent almost two years trying to get a new automated warehouse system running, and it is still nowhere near living up to the initial expectations."

"Sounds like a case of being once bitten, twice shy," said Alexander. "Well, all we can do is to set out the business case as best we can and hope the benefits are clear enough to overcome the reservations."

HOW NOT TO CONVINCE A SKEPTIC

The conversation gnawed away at Alexander in the final days leading up to the meeting. Fear of failure is a strong motivator to do nothing, and fear is not normally something that can be overcome with cold facts. Fear is an emotion, and strong emotions tend not to listen too closely to rational argument. Previous experiences that Alexander had had made him think that when you came up against a hardened skeptic, the very worst thing you could do was to bombard them with facts and figures in order to convince them.

Alexander's firm practiced the whole presentation the day before the meeting. His boss spent a large part of the day working out potential objections the client might have and how they would deal with them. "We need to squash any objection that comes up, so we need all the evidence that we might need right there in the room," he said. "There will be no second chances on this one."

> *Fear is an emotion.*

The minute Alexander's team walked into the meeting room, he could sense that things were not looking good. His champion shook hands with him but barely made eye contact, and then sat down quickly at the far end of the meeting room. Even before everyone had settled into their seats, some of the client team were talking amongst themselves about another meeting on a different subject to take place later that day. Their mind was already on a different subject. There were no negative comments, but every part of their body language and behavior was pointing the wrong way.

THIS MIGHT NOT WORK FOR YOU

After a few minutes of introduction Alexander was asked to open up the meeting. He took a deep breath that felt more like a sigh and looked down at the notes they had so carefully prepared. Then he looked at the members of the client team whom he knew were the most skeptical about the project and made a decision.

"Thank you all for making the time for this meeting and for giving us so much support over the past few weeks in helping us to put together our proposal," he said. "We have a ton of information we want to share with you, and as you might imagine it points to the conclusion that you should buy our solution." A few people in the room laughed gently and most smiled at the openness of his comment.

"But one thing we all need to accept is that there is a strong possibility that this will not make sense for you right now. There are a lot of obstacles in the way. It will take quite a lot of commitment and, to be honest, stamina to make this happen." Everyone in the room was now giving Alexander 100 percent of their attention.

> *"Could you help me understand where you all see the biggest risks in this project?"*

"On our side, we are convinced that we can deliver what we promise. Because we rehearsed this whole presentation yesterday, I am confident that we can back up our belief with hard facts. The issue here of course is that this project will be disruptive to your organization—there is a lot of change involved here. There are also risks. The main thing we don't know yet is whether you as an organization feel that this all makes sense."

Alexander could see that everyone in the room was now fully engaged, especially his boss who was staring openly at Alexander with something approaching a look of shock on his face.

"If you don't mind me asking," continued Alexander, "could you help me understand where you all see the biggest risks in this project? Where could it go wrong?"

UNCOVERING BOOBY TRAPS

After what seemed like a long silence, a member of the client team who was known to be skeptical of the project piped up. "If you don't bring the production teams along with you, then you would struggle to get them to buy into making the changes this project would need. People have seen a few big projects being started that never worked out, so there is big internal sale required for the manufacturing department."

Alexander's firm had previously worked successfully with a change management consultancy on just this sort of issue, so after a few minutes of discussion he walked over to a flip chart and wrote: "Change management program for production teams."

"I can only imagine there must be other potential obstacles we would need to deal with together," he said.

Another member of the client team who had so far shown no real involvement in the initiative spoke up. "There is a lot of suspicion about these big ideas within our people," he said. "There tends to be a pile of work at the early stages, with benefits only to be delivered at some distant point in the future."

Alexander asked for some examples and then tried to summarize, writing on the flip chart, "Must establish early win with clear results in the early stages."

By now the meeting was starting to focus, initially on problems but then quickly on how to resolve them. The flip chart had several headline issues and a one-line description of what would have to happen to make them work. None of them were deal breakers, but some of them were news to Alexander's team.

ANYTHING ELSE?

After almost an hour of this, Alexander looked at his watch and spoke to the group. "Can I ask if we have covered all the major issues on this? We would like to know if we have missed anything."

After a moment's silence one of the most senior managers from the client team responded. "I think we have covered all the critical points here. My question to you is, do you think you can handle them?"

Alexander looked at his boss for support, and then said, "Obviously we need to look at these in more detail, but based on other projects we have done of this size I would say that we can get back to you with a revised proposal that can cover these requirements within two weeks. If we do that, do you think we can all make this happen to your original schedule?" He looked directly at the most skeptical member of the client team when he said this.

> *"Can I ask if we have covered all the major issues?"*

"If you can show us how you can do this in a way that we can afford, then I can't see any reason why we can't," the skeptic said.

The meeting broke up with the intention to meet again in two weeks and a clear commitment to move forward if the issues raised had a workable plan to resolve them.

THE BOSS'S TURN TO SPEAK

When they reached the parking lot outside the office, Alexander's boss said, "We spent days working on that presentation and never showed a single slide. That took some nerve." Alexander held his breath for a moment, waiting for what came next. "It was a great meeting, and you made the right call," said his boss. "Good effort."

Over the next two weeks Alexander and his team reached out to most of the people from the client side who had been at the meeting. He described to each how his team was going to address the challenges raised in the meeting, to make sure that the solutions would be workable. When the whole group reassembled, the project was given a green light.

SANDLER TAKEAWAYS FOR BOOTSTRAPPERS

1. **Selling is not a simple case of doing things by the numbers.** Sometimes it needs the intelligent willingness to accept risk. The ability to behave in a fearless manner is the toughest but most effective behavior in a bootstrapper.

2. **The problem the prospect discusses is never the real problem.** The issue that needed to be overcome in this example was not technical; it was organizational. To get a prospect to discuss this openly requires a relationship of equality and a visible commitment to solving a problem, not just a plan to make a sale.

3. **The best sales presentation is the one you never give.** The more you prepare, the stronger your chance of success. Yet sales is not about simply presenting smart projector slides. You have the responsibility to own the process, and that means to be willing and able to respond bravely to changes in the sales situation and to focus on the people in front of you rather than just the technical content of your offering.

4. **People like to do business with people they like.** How you act during the sales process is viewed by your prospects as an indicator of how you will act when you actually deliver. If you sell by being open, honest, and focused on solving the pains the prospect has, you create the impression that you care about generating value for them, not just a sale for yourself.

EPILOGUE

Of all the "rules" that David Sandler established for sales, the one that resonates the most for me is: "There are no bad prospects, only bad salespeople." For a long time I struggled with that; after all, I had met dozens of prospects and customers in my life who seemed worse than bad. They seemed terrible!

In reality, I had met plenty of people who did not qualify to be my customers. They had no pain that I could solve, or they could not find the budget to fix their problems. That didn't make them bad prospects; it meant that they were not a good fit for me and my offerings. I had allowed myself to fall into the trap in which the only acceptable response to my sales pitches was a *yes*.

There is no blame for getting a *no* in sales—in fact, it is often the best answer you can hear. I should have figured that out for myself. I had also come across my fair share of people who cut meetings short, ignored my calls, pumped me for endless free consulting or acted in a generally unacceptable way. But the problem was not their behavior; it was my failure to control the situation.

As I was learning the Sandler way of selling, I had to accept that, time and again, the problems I had experienced in my sales career came down to the fact that I either said or did something I shouldn't have, or I didn't say or do something I should have.

The difference between being a business-building, bootstrapping, entrepreneurial sales professional and someone who goes through life saying things like, "At least I am not the worst in the world," is that the bootstrapper steps up and accepts that his sales destiny is not in the hand of the prospect.

I wrote this book with one intention: to show that, in any sales situation, the only variable you can control is your own behavior. To drive that behavior, you need to put yourself in the position of being the one making the decisions. At every step in the sales process and during every discussion with a client, you can keep your focus on how you decide to behave.

Take the responsibility to behave in a way that is intelligent... or fearless...or flexible...or fun. Maybe all four at the same time. That's the best-case scenario for bootstrappers. And that's the kind of career I wish for you as a bootstrapping salesperson.

Look for these other books
on Amazon.com:

Prospect the Sandler Way

Transforming Leaders the Sandler Way

Selling Professional Services the Sandler Way

Accountability the Sandler Way

Selling Technology the Sandler Way

LinkedIn the Sandler Way

CONGRATULATIONS!

Bootstrap Selling the Sandler Way
includes a complimentary seminar!

Take this opportunity to personally experience the non-traditional sales training and reinforcement coaching that has been recognized internationally for decades.

Companies in the Fortune 1000 as well as thousands of small- to medium-sized businesses choose Sandler for sales, leadership, management, and a wealth of other skill-building programs. Now, it's your turn, and it's free!

You'll learn the latest practical, tactical, feet-in-the-street sales methods directly from your neighborhood Sandler trainers! They're knowledgeable, friendly, and informed about your local selling environment.

Here's how you redeem YOUR FREE SEMINAR invitation.

1. Go to www.Sandler.com and click on Find Training Location (top blue bar).
2. Select your location.
3. Review the list of all the Sandler trainers in your area.
4. Call your local Sandler trainer, mention *Bootstrap Selling the Sandler Way,* and reserve your place at the next seminar!